The Second Coming

NR

The Second Coming

You Are the Christ

Markus Ray

Foreword by
Sondra Ray

Immortal Ray Productions
Nashville Washington D.C.

IMMORTAL RAY PRODUCTIONS
301 TINGEY STREET, SE
WASHINGTON DC, 20003

Immortal Ray Productions
Nashville Washington D.C.

Library Of Congress Cataloging in Publication Data

Ray, Markus; The Second Coming

I. Spiritual Life. 2. Conduct of life. 3. Life Purpose

All quotes from *A Course in Miracles* are from the 3rd Edition published by The Foundation For Inner Peace, authorized by it's scribe, Dr. Helen Schucman

Cover Design: Markus Ray
Frontispiece: "Jesus of Poland" by Markus Ray
Foreword and Afterword by Sondra Ray
Back Cover Image: Judy Totton Photography of London.

ISBN 13: Paperback 978-1-950684-06-9
ISBN 13: E-Book 978-1-950684-07-6

Dedication

I dedicate this book to all of you, my readers, with whom I AM ONE. We will get this together, or not at all. In these times of global challenges, we will rise up together and Love each other with an unconditional love, or not at all. Together we make this journey to be the Christ, our undaunted and immaculate Self. The world needs us, we who are taking up this life purpose, we who yearn to know our holiness, beyond all the "made up" versions of who we already thought we were. May we hold hands together in this journey. May we laugh and cry in the brilliance of His Love, that shines on Everything. *The Second Coming* is dedicated to you, because You are the Christ; and your entry into my life, you who are touching this book and reading it, is my greatest joy.

Markus Ray

Washington D.C.
Navy Yard
14—March—2020

A Meditation for Times of Trouble:
14—MAR—2020

I call upon God's Name and on my own.
(ACIM; Workbook; Lesson # 183)

1. May the Power of Christ blanket you.
2. May the Blanket of Christ protect you.
3. May the Protection of Christ calm you.
4. May the Calmness of Christ still you.
5. May the Stillness of Christ awaken you.
6. May the Awakened Christ bless you.
7. May the Blessed Christ give you peace.
8. May the Peaceful Christ give certainty.
9. May the Certain Christ resolve all things.
10. May the Resolute Christ help you.
11. May the Helpful Christ give you solutions.
12. May the Solution of Christ bring you joy.
13. May the Joyful Christ uplift your hearts.
14. May the Uplifted Christ shine on you.
15. May the Shining Christ brighten you.
16. May the Brightened Christ show you.
17. May the Showing Christ lead your way.
18. May the Leading Christ simplify your life.
19. May the Simple Christ solve your problem.
20. May the Solution of Christ bring clarity.
21. May the Clear Christ show you the way.
22. May the Way of Christ be your rock.
23. May the Rock of Christ give you strength.
24. May the Strength of Christ make you mighty.
25. May the Mighty Christ give you relief.
26. May the Relieving Christ help you relax.
27. May the Relaxing Christ descend upon you.
28. May the Descended Christ engulf your being.
29. May the Engulfing Christ surround you fully.
30. May the Surrounding Christ shelter you.

Christ's Second Coming, which is sure as God, is merely the correction of mistakes, and the return of sanity. It is a part of the condition that restores the never lost, and re-establishes what is forever and forever true. It is the invitation to God's Word to take illusion's place; the willingness to let forgiveness rest upon all things without exception and without reserve.

(From A Course in Miracles, Workbook, The Second Coming, the Preamble to Lessons 301-310)

Contents

PART 4

PART 5

Foreword

I just want to say how absolutely wonderful it is to be married to someone so devoted to *A Course in Miracles* like Markus is. I feel I have an enlightened marriage because of this. We are both committed to it and the process of mutual growth, sharing a common goal of service to God.

Markus has actually memorized all the 365 lessons in *ACIM* and the great thing is he will sit and meditate and say them to himself. I find this so amazing! His Love is pure because he has surrendered the old way of thinking. He is always affirming that Love is our priority in every situation. This is what *ACIM* teaches, and he practices it regularly. Because of this, he can actualize the power of God. Love in his mind produces Love in our life. To me, his mind is like an altar to God. For this reason, he can be a clear poet, artist, and writer. Sometimes he comes out of the bathroom and is channeling something that *ACIM* would totally agree with. He really lives the lesson, "I am willing to see things differently." He always gives me and others his divine Love. His mind is a vessel for divine Love. He always works toward the highest level of good for everyone involved in any situation. So in this way, he is what *ACIM* asks us to become—a miracle worker.

Because he has let the past go, he is not contaminating the present in any way. He sees every situation we find ourselves in as an opportunity. Because he has worked out his anger, our relationship is very peaceful. He does not judge me or find fault. He pretty much is non-reactive to the external. He really sees me and others through God's eyes. The ego is always saying, "What can I get?" Markus is always saying, "What can I give?" He does not try to hide his weaknesses either and he knows our relationship is a context for healing so we don't suppress our blocks to Love. We work them out together. Our holy relationship is a context where we can be ourselves. We don't judge each other's shadows if they come up. I feel he has written this book to expand your heart and to help you become more deeply Loving.

What qualifies Markus to write a book about *A Course in Miracles*? Not only does he live it; but more importantly, he is in the direct lineage from where it came. He studied for 17 years with the Master Teacher, Tara Singh, who trained directly under Dr. Helen Schucman, who scribed the book from Jesus Himself.

Markus's teacher, Tara Singh, spent three whole years in silence before he started teaching *ACIM*. He had been a student of Krishnamurti for over twenty-five years when he met Helen Schucman, so he was able to recognize her as a fully enlightened soul. He would easily surrender to her. Dr. Schucman was a psychologist and educator who happened to be a very lofty soul, even at the level of Mother Mary, it was said. "Mary gave birth to Jesus's body, and Dr. Schucman gave birth to Jesus's mind." So because Markus was directly taught in the way that kept the lineage pure, he can explain *ACIM* better than most. He tells about his 17-year journey with Tara Singh in his first book, *Miracles with My Master, Tara Singh*. And more recently he wrote more extensively about the relationship between Krishnamurti, Dr. Schucman, and Tara Singh in his book called *The Master Is Beautiful*.

A Course in Miracles says that *The Second Coming* is the end of the ego's rule. That is when we trade in the mind of the ego for the mind of the Holy Spirit. It is "merely the correction of mistakes and the return to sanity." That is enlightenment. There are steps to take in this process of moving out of the ego's mindset of "mistakes" into the Holy Spirit's "love of correction." This book can take you through them. You will be caressed and guided through a deeper understanding of *A Course in Miracles* in your life. When all is said and done, this book can introduce you to a closer relationship with Jesus, a fully enlightened Being. Therefore Markus is taking you on a path to enlightenment—and what could be higher than that?

A Course in Miracles is a roadmap to your Higher Self, to your Christ Self. And Markus's *The Second Coming* is a helpful guide which makes sure you don't miss the signs along the way. He has been through the *Course* many times. He has a vast background with Tara Singh that gives added Energy to what he shares. When Lesson #296 says, "The Holy Spirit speaks through me today," Markus is listening, and then he is speaking what he hears. This is a practice we all must make in the end. Are we living and being guided through our Divine Connections, or are we just blundering along, thinking we are on the right track when we are lost in a wilderness of detours of our own making, and the uncertainty of human doubt?

The choice is always ours to wake up and have the ears to hear. How long will we wait? How much more time will we waste? *The Second Coming* is upon us. Markus is here to awaken himself and you in the process of fully accepting this fact. We are ascending together in the Christ or not at all. Why not join us in this Ascension? What better thing do we have to do with our life?

LOVE, Sondra Ray

Preface

Christ has come again on this very day, in *A Course in Miracles*. This makes us truly blessed in this modern age! I am writing this book to help people wake up to this fact, and help myself wake up to this fact. There is Pure Joy in being our highest God created Self. I am writing this book to introduce more people to *A Course in Miracles* and its teachings, which is nothing short of *the Second Coming* of the Christ into our midst and into our minds.

Humanity has known about Jesus the Christ for 2000 years. We have built religions and great churches around this knowledge. Recently in Cologne, I walked into the grand Cathedral there which took over 632 years to complete. It allegedly houses the bones of the Three Kings who paid their adoration to the Christ Child. The building stands as a testament to His great miracles and deeds—nothing short of resurrecting from the dead—yet the actuality of experiencing these kinds of miracles in our own lives evades us. Why are we not resurrecting from the dead? A Teacher's teachings should be transforming us from within. Even Jesus told his disciples, "And greater works shall ye do."

This transformation within us does not mean we cannot receive inspiration from the past structures we built to honor the Christ. Yet, we need a new standard of reasoning that says, "To the degree we are living as the Christ, and being a witness to the miracles made accessible through Him, we have a greater need—*The Second Coming* of Him into our hearts and minds." We must think differently. We must see differently. We must live differently. We must *be* different.

Miraculously, the Cologne Cathedral withstood 37,711 tons of bombs dropped on the city by the Allies in World War II. But many human beings did not. Twenty thousand people of Cologne were killed—men, women, and children—who were not necessarily combatants (Wikipedia-Bombing of Cologne). We are all amazed at the fact the Cathedral is still standing. Yet, what about the 20,000 people killed? Arguments are made to justify the inhumanity of man to man in a wartime setting, but what about the wars going on in our relationships—and in ourselves—in our families—in our workplaces and environments that are psychologically raging?

Christ glorified in a structure like the Cologne Cathedral has endured in our memory over twenty centuries, but where is He in the edifice of our own hearts? Have we withstood the bombing of indifference that accepts these cruelties as the collateral damage of human progress? Or do we see the actual travesty that two cultures, so very much touting that "God is on our side," could engage so utterly in destroying one another?

I was born on 11-11-1954, less than 10 years after the bombing of Cologne stopped. November 11^{th,} 1918 was honored as "Armistice Day," for on that day the treaty was signed to end the fighting of World War I. Some notion that I had a purpose to "end war" was always hovering around my birthday. The "war to end all wars" was fought. Some estimates are 17,000,000 souls died in the conflict. In WW II, less than 25 years later, some estimates say 85,000,000 people perished, five times as many than lost in the "war to end all wars." So much for "Armistice Day."

Somehow we, as a human race, have separated ourselves from the Source of Love, producing a cataclysm of human tragedy. Christ is just as much needed now as in the times of the Roman Empire. He comes into an insane picture of the downside of human endeavors. Fortunately for us, God sent His Teacher. Again. Why would He not come again to counteract the dark forces that seem to grip and control the psyche of modern man? We need a mind shift here. We need to divert the military-industrial complex to the "Love your neighbor complex." Governments of the most powerful nations on earth need to start trusting each other, and helping their own people first, and then using their surplus to help other developing nations. We need a miracle here—and it has come. We need to accept and allow it into manifestation.

The Second Coming came in the form of *A Course in Miracles* in 1965 to a Jewish psychology practitioner and professor at Colombia University in New York City. Many of us "New Agers" are well familiar with this action. Marianne Williamson and Oprah Winfrey, Gary Renard and Gerald Jampolsky—all these are the popular mouthpieces of this great and stupendous modern-day scripture. Yet is was Tara Singh, my Teacher, who had a direct relationship with the scribe, Dr. Helen Schucman. She had not only received *The Second Coming* of Jesus and written it down, and functioned as the "mother of Christ's Mind," but she also had transformed Tara Singh by giving him an awareness of his Christ Self. This miracle took place almost totally unrecognized, just as *A Course in Miracles* is still treated as another "new age book." People say, "Oh, Yes, I read the thing twenty years ago." Well, unless they were awakened to *be the Christ* in their life now, they did not *really* read it at all.

A Course in Miracles has been in our midst for over forty years. What will we do in the next forty years to bring it into application in our lives? We are challenged to bring a Truth into practice so an inner transformation can take place in us. *ACIM* can certainly transform us as individuals, and more broadly as a human race. It is nothing short of the Christ's *Second Coming*. Through it, the Christ is among us. Do we even care? Will we give these sacred words their deserved attention?

Jesus said He would "come again." We took that to mean another incarnation of the Christ—meaning in another human form. We did not think that the "second coming" would be one of an Idea, a Thought standing on its own without the accompanied person in a body of flesh and bone. This is what He did, though. He "came again" in America, as a Thought in the Mind of God to these physical planes, *without a body*. He came and remains here, and will stay here indefinitely, in fact forever, as long as the human race is present, in the true words of *A Course in Miracles*.

2000 years prior, Jesus brought His message of Love, Peace, and Joy. He extended forgiveness to His "enemies" who crucified Him to set the precedent for His resurrection from "death." He ascended into the very real Immortal Realms of the Divine Source of Life. He released us from judgments through the main tenets of His teaching. He "saved us" from the personal "hell" we made through complete forgiveness, which He called the Atonement. A great force of religion built up around Him over the centuries. This we all know and can observe.

We also observe that strife, wars, struggles, and violence have been justified in His name and that somehow these justifications, and projections of "guilt" onto the oppressed, were inconsistent with His life and message. Therefore many of us left the churches of our childhood and sought a more pure version of spiritual truths through our own explorations. We left organized religion but maintained our yearnings to know God, to know Truth, to know a Higher Principle to live by—and even to know the Christ directly, not through a *middle man*.

America's ideals are Freedom of religion; Freedom of speech; Freedom to pursue Life, Liberty, and Happiness in ways that sing to our individual souls. We want to be Free more than anything else. But somehow we observe we are not free. We feel depressed, conflicted within, often butting up against an invisible system that is complex and can be indifferent to our needs. We feel pressured to keep up. The bills roll in, and we attempt to keep ahead of the productive curve to produce a *better bottom line*. The success gurus write another book. We buy it, read it, and seem to remain the same. Then we ask ourselves, "There must be another way to live?"

Enter in *The Second Coming*. Dr. Helen Schucman was the first to whom Jesus was to come. Over the periods of her scribing *A Course in Miracles* from 1965 to 1972, she went through a deep inner transformation in which the Christ awakened her to her true Christ Self. Dr. Schucman was as pure as Mary. Mary gave birth to Jesus's body; Holy Helen gave birth to Jesus's Mind. One could say she was a Divine Mother, American style.

This is the Destiny of America, to be the harbinger of *the Second Coming*. The instant Dr. Schucman started writing down the Thoughts of the Christ, *the Second Coming* was taking place. Fulfilling a long-awaited Destiny, America entered into its "fifth wave" of Freedom. The first was the American Revolution. The second was the Civil War and the abolishment of slavery. The third was its triumph in WWI&II over world fascism. And fourthly, we had the movement to end racial and gender inequality that began in the 1960s. The fifth is the Freedom bestowed on us by the Mind of God, independent of national governments or church cannons, that transcends all external systems of *laws* altogether.

My teacher Tara Singh called *A Course in Miracles* "A Gift for All Mankind." The Gift has been given. I write this book to assure it is publicly known on a larger scale, as a major guide to the people in America and around the world. The true Destiny of America is to be the facilitator of this *Second Coming*. And this book is the roadmap for its purpose and practice.

The Christ is in you, my reader. You are the Christ. The Second Coming is your awakening to this fact. May this book be *truly helpful* in your process of awakening. May it remove your struggles and lighten your load. May it bring you the inner Peace and Joy of miracles.

Markus Ray

The Navy Yards
Washington D.C.

Acknowledgments

I could not have written this book without my Holy Relationship with three people. First, with Sondra Ray, my wife, whom I met around 1985 in a Loving Relationships Training in Philadelphia. When she said, "*A Course in Miracles* is the most important book written in 2000 years," I was hooked. Then in 1989 I met a man, Tara Singh, my Spiritual Master Teacher of *ACIM*, who further shook my world. "I have nothing to teach," he said, "you know too much already." That began a seventeen year journey of undoing my ego, and anything else of my "knowing too much" that was standing in the way of me being my true Self. The third Holy relationship was with my ex-wife, Sue Sipos, with whom I spent 30 years. She gave me some of the best years of her life, as I did for her, and for this I will be forever grateful. As destiny would have it, we both reached a point where it was clear that *God had other lessons for us to learn.* Without her, I would not have been so focused on my spiritual life. We are both artists. And artists, by their very nature, are spiritual beings. This *awakening of the spirit* was always in the first place for Sue and me while we were together. Thank You, Sue. You are forever in my heart.

Those on the practical side: I would like to thank Barbara Milbourn in advance. She is my *editor in the wings*. It is a relationship of the heart. I would like to thank Amazon.com for giving independent writers the full control of their work, unencumbered, to speak their truth to the universe. I would like to thank Apple, Inc. for my MacBook Pro. We have a holy relationship, my "Mac and Me." Only other Mac users can understand. "Once you go Mac, you never go back," I always say. In this department I also would like to thank Martin Thomas, my Mac "guru," who turned me on to the thing in the first place in 2008. He fixes all my glitches, holds my hand through crashes, and nags me with the perennial question of safe practices—"Did you back-up?"

Those I never met, to whom I am indebted: Dr. Helen Schucman and Mr. J. Krishnamurti were my "Teacher's Teachers." They shaped Tara Singh to awaken into his *God Created Self.* Without them the clarity would not have flowed freely through Tara Singh to me. I honor them in my lineage as Essential Lights. I wrote about them in *The Master Is Beautiful*. They are Great Rays. I bow at their feet, even though they would never want me to, because I saw through Tara Singh their greater wisdom.

No book I write would go without acknowledging Sri Haidakhan Babaji, the immortal yogi Christ of India. He is my wife Sondra Ray's Master. He as well guides our life in ways that are far beyond thought. He is the Master of the Masters. Even Jesus is said to have studied with Him in India 2000 years ago. We bow at His feet every Spring on the India Quest, and practice His teachings of Truth, Simplicity, Love and Service.

And last but not least, to those I will meet in the future, my readers: little do we know the workings of the Divine. But this I know—those whom we meet we are predestined to meet. Every encounter is Holy, with the great potential of Miracles. We cannot love God without loving every human being first. I love God through loving YOU, my reader. I acknowledge you first and foremost in this book, *The Second Coming*, to be the Christ in my life. May we together rise to meet Him in ourselves.

Introduction

What is the Christ? This question is put to us by the wise. Two thousand years of church history and dogma have not seemed to give us much inner peace and real connection to the answer. But we are still pondering His miracles even now, so long after their performance, especially resurrecting Himself from the dead. Now Jesus has *come again*, and this book is intended to lead us to an effulgent vision of this fact. *The Second Coming* of the Christ is upon us, and Jesus is sitting in front of you ready to have a conversation.

But before I get into that more deeply, a little something about myself, and my relationship with Jesus and the church. It was mostly my mother, Elizabeth, who took my sister and me to church. Most Sundays we went to the Mount Vernon, Ohio, Gay Street United Methodist Church growing up. Grandma was very involved as well. She was a member of the Eastern Star, the ladies auxiliary section of the Masons. Dad and Grandpa stayed home most of the time. They were probably tired from working all week. Mother and Grandma worked too, but they had more of a yearning to put God in our life, and make the worship of Jesus an important principle in our world. Carol and I would go to Sunday school, then meet Mom and Grandma in the Sanctuary for the Sunday Service after our class.

I liked the songs and the spaciousness of the Sanctuary. The stained glass windows above the choir loft in the eastern apse of the church were spectacular. Also, the red carpet running down the central aisle was memorable. And people wore robes—the ministers and the choir members. Deep purple robes emitted an aura of spectacular character. When the minister would give his speech I would listen, but usually, halfway through it I would fall asleep and Mom would be nudging me to stay awake. Then there would be a new song to sing, and we would have to stand, so I would be wide awake again.

Then when the music reached a great crescendo, men in suits and ties came up the central aisle from the back, passing gold plates at every pew. This was very impressionable on a little kid, with all that money in the plates as they passed by, as we added our few dollars. Mom often put a sealed envelope in the golden offering plate, so I never knew how much money she was actually putting in there. Sometimes she let me put in a few quarters, and sometimes a dollar. This was in the 1960s when I suspect our money was worth more.

Sunday school taught us to be good, and treat your neighbor as yourself like you would want to be treated; don't lie or steal; study hard in school; mind your parents—stuff like that. When all was said and done, what I really looked forward to from Sunday School were the little *Match Box* cars my teacher would give us boys when we memorized something like *The Lord's Prayer* from the Bible. And after church, I loved our trip down to the Mount Vernon city square, only a few blocks away, where I could see the large goldfish in the fountain there. Mom would buy us a Fanny Farmer mint chocolate bar in the local drug store on the corner. It was the smoothest chocolate ever made, I can recall.

Later in my life, the question remained. What is the Christ? What actual role does He play in my life? What real connection do I have with Him that is in the present, not based on historic speculation? I never officially "joined" the Methodist church. Because Dad was a Catholic, I was actually baptized in the Catholic Church, where my Aunt Vera from Brooklyn stood up for me as my God-Mother. I considered myself a Christian, but even that was a bit distant when I went away to art school in Cleveland when I was 18. The big city was a shock to me, and art school even more. I was from a small town in central Ohio going to the cultural section of Cleveland, called *University Circle,* which was an oasis of University and cultural institutions in an otherwise ghetto-like situation. Well, Life is a long meander. Eventually, I ended up at the Tyler School of Art in Philadelphia to get my Master's Degree in Art.

In Philadelphia, I met up with the metaphysical community there in the form of Sondra Ray and Rebirthing in the mid-1980s. It was a great time. Sondra introduced me to *A Course in Miracles,* and my interest in the Christ was rekindled. She said, "This is the most important book written in two thousand years," and that got my attention. I studied it for a few years and could not put it down.

And then in 1989 I met Tara Singh who was speaking on this modern-day scripture at Stony Point, New York. I was floored by him. He stunned me to the core of my being with the sheer force of his truth. I guess all the years I went to church with Mom paid off, because I could listen to him give his talk—like it was a sermon, but not like a sermon—and this time stay completely awake and attentive. Every word that came out of him went directly into my heart like a shot of adrenalin. I felt as though I was *being revived*. Not only was I super awake after hearing him for the first time, I could hardly believe I had so much to undo in myself—so much that was hard-fought to obtain. My identity was rendered mostly meaningless. It was *an image of myself* whom Tara Singh had just exposed as my false self of the ego I *made up*.

I wrote this book in five parts as my exploration of the impact *A Course in Miracles,* and Tara Singh's presentation of it had on me. Also, I wrote it to help people *meet the Christ* in themselves.

❖

PART 1 is simply called, "What Is the Christ?" These are the chapters:

1. The Mind's Power
2. The Known Is Past
3. Freedom Is Present
4. Christ Is the Link
5. Total Forgiveness

I knew from Sondra Ray that my thoughts were the ruler of my "reality," and these thoughts have power. I am responsible for making up my world and my experiences with my thoughts. But when I met Tara Singh I went to a place in the mind that was beyond thought. He spoke of a still Mind, a silent mind. This I had not approached so closely before. In the course of his lectures, he could bring the minds of the people in the audience to this stillness—to this *silence within.* This Easter weekend of 1989 began my 17-year tutelage with Tara Singh. I was with him as a student until he passed in 2006. I consider myself his student still, as he had the *Light of Christ* flowing through him, and I was the beneficiary of this Light that shines to this day in me. The power of the Mind to free itself of relative thought is mostly about letting go of the past. When we are not preoccupied with past thoughts, we can have a creative purpose in life. What is our purpose upon the planet? We all eventually have to answer this for ourselves. Tara Singh got me in touch with that purpose.

Since 1985, when Sondra Ray introduced me to *A Course in Miracles,* the *Course* has been a very central part of my life. I recognized it as my main spiritual practice, my *sadhana,* as they say in India. But I also knew I needed a teacher, a Master, to make its truth an actuality in my Life. What we know is mostly from the past, and this knowledge is limited. It is partial, and we are seeking to be whole, based on it. But knowledge can never be complete—as much as we try to *learn more.* We are chasing a carrot we never achieve, but somehow think if we keep chasing it we will end up more satisfied. But the past accumulations of experience and knowledge never fulfill us. What then, do we do?

Freedom is in the present, the great spiritual teachers make this clear. And what is in the present is already here, not needing any learning, or accomplishment, or belief, or system of thought to justify it. Love is in the present, and it is all-pervading. You cannot "learn it," nor achieve it. It does not come from you. It is what the philosophers, the "lovers of wisdom," call *a priori*—pre-existing. Christ is merely the being who is in touch with this Love, in the present, having freed Himself of all of the judgments and worn-out memories of the past. He is in a state of total release from the past through forgiveness. His forgiveness is complete. In the present, He has no grievances nor discontent. He is in a state of Constant Joy without any deviation from that Joy. He is in the awareness of his Divine Self-Identity. He is the link with a Self we share. He connects us to one another and God. He transcends human form, yet is also immersed in human form. He is connected to Nature, and to the Cosmic Forces of the Universe. He knows no bounds because He remains forever joined to the Mind of God, which is Infinity Itself. He is *in us*, and we are *in Him.*

This might sound like lofty, highfalutin stuff. You might say, "So what. I don't feel free of the past in my life, nor am I in a state of constant Joy. What does the Christ have to do with me?" Well, most of us have a lot of work to do to let go of our past. It is lodged in the deep recesses of our minds and persists like an indelible scar on the mental pathways of our life. Our family, relatives, and ancestors handed their best and brightest down to us, but they also gave us their shadows and conundrums. And we accepted them unaware we were even doing that. We inherited the dark side of our character, apparently to forgive and undo it in this lifetime, once and for all. And we picked a family that was optimum for these lessons of forgiveness.

❖

Forgiveness is the work we must do. **PART 2** discusses this work. The Work Required :

6. Who Do We Hate?
7. The Law of Love
8. The Work of Forgiveness
9. The Gifts of God
10. Love of Correction

There is a lot of undoing necessary to be free of judgments and opinions. Who do we hate? We all have had someone in our life who pushed the boundaries of likeability in our book. They *pushed our buttons* big time. Maybe there was a misunderstanding; maybe more, some physical or sexual abuse; or someone stole from us; even worse, someone inflicted violence upon us. Whatever the infraction, someone is in our mind now whom we have deemed evil, and we have cut them out of the realm of goodness we reserve for everyone else. We "love to hate them." Are we willing to see them as our "savior" instead of our enemy? Are we willing to see there was something in our subconscious mental vibration that pulled them into our experience? We attracted that person (and their behavior) into our life for some very important lesson we are to get. This is part of the major work to do in accepting *The Second Coming*. We are responsible for their "acts against us," and in reality, they are here to teach us forgiveness.

There is a "law of Love" which says, "What we give out we will get back." If we put out anger, judgments, and resentment, we will receive back the same from others. If we put out forgiveness, compassion and the vision that all people have a core of goodness in themselves, we will receive back people treating us in that way. In other words, the writer Esther Hicks calls this the "law of Attraction." We will attract a *match* to our inner vibration on our emotional scale. This is neither "good" nor "bad," it is just a law. What is our vibration? It is an exact match for the people and the results we are getting in our life. Sondra Ray puts it this way, "Our thoughts are creative." We create everything in our life with our thoughts. Thoughts precede all of our experiences. We have experiences according to our thoughts. Feelings are spearheaded by thoughts as well.

How do we raise our vibration and change our thoughts? It is all up to us. If someone makes us angry, then obviously they are triggering that in us. The thing they did to trigger us is one thing, but the anger we hold toward them is our responsibility. How do we transmute that energy back to the inner peace of Pure Joy? Forgiveness is the only means. And this is not "letting another off the hook" because we are feeling so self-righteous. This is in the seeing that our "vibrational match" to the situation created it—or attracted it. We are responsible for all that comes to us. It is the beginning of real forgiveness. It's not a heavy thing either. We are relieved of our judgments and concerns, which makes us free of the past. It puts us in the present, where all the fun is! Which would we rather have? Past condemnation or present happiness? The true work of forgiveness puts us in the Present Happiness of *Now* while pardoning all of the rest.

In the *Now* are what Jesus calls the *Gifts of God.* These gifts are very simple, but also very beautiful. They are states of Mind that will envelop our life, and transform all around us into a Heaven on Earth. They will clarify our purpose for being here on earth. They will blanket our perception to be one of peace and joy, and erase the tendencies to be stuck in struggle and conflict. So much energy will flow into us from the *Gifts of God* that we will be different people after really receiving them. Not to say we will "lose ourselves," but we will be the Self we always desired to be, effortlessly, without any *becoming something else*. We will just be ourselves as we have never fully been before—and this will be amazingly *different*.

The *love of correction* is something Tara Singh stressed to the students who worked closely with him. It says in the introduction of *ACIM* that the meaning of Love is far beyond our limited definitions, but it does say the purpose of the curriculum is to "remove the blocks to the awareness of Love's presence." This would entail a *love of correction*. This is what removing blocks is. It is a deep process of introspection and taking responsibility for all of our results in life, and changing the thought factors in us which have produced painful or undesirable results. Sondra Ray has a saying, "Your results are your gurus." This means, if we don't like what's happening in our life, we have to find out "what is in us," those thoughts in our mind that resulted in the situation we don't like—and then change our mind. This process of inner transformation is called *the love of correction*.

❖

What is this actual entry of the Christ in this age, and into our life? **PART 3** discusses The Second Coming. How does it unfold? These are the chapters that describe this process.

11. Life Purpose
12. Living as the Christ
13. Rebooting Our Life
14. Stepping Out of Fear
15. Embracing Love

The Second Coming of Jesus is merely the *awareness of the truth* that He is already here. It is said best by Jesus Himself here:

> *The Second Coming is the awareness of reality, not its return—Behold, my child, reality is here. It belongs to you and me and God, and is perfectly satisfying to all of us. Only this awareness heals, because it is the awareness of truth.*
>
> *(ACIM; Chapter 9; Section IV; ¶ 10-11)*

Do we have a clear grasp of our Life Purpose, and the awareness of the truth of that? An awareness of Unconditional Love would be a lofty goal for us all to embrace. Think of the wisdom of this—if all the governments of the world, and the people who compose them, embraced this higher truth of Love. The function of Unconditional Love is Constant Happiness. The governments may not change with their agendas, but the individual can—and must change. *The Second Coming* is living as the Christ in our daily life. It is a reality already here, but we have to shift our life's purpose to embrace it. We have to *live it* in a state of Pure Joy.

We have to reboot our life to *live as the Christ*. This amounts to rebooting our minds. The mind rules our life. It is like a computer program. How have we programmed it? Is there an original *Divine Default System* that God put there? It seems we have added so much of our own unnecessary, problematic, virus-ridden content, we need to have a complete cleanout and reboot of our mental *program* to arrive back at our *Divine Default System*. This is the thought system of the Holy Spirit, which is also the Mind of the Christ, the *program of Absolute Love*.

Notice how this might bring up some fear of reading this. All our former rejections of fundamentalist religions may come up. All our fears of *sacrificing ourselves* may come up. All our anger about God "not being here" for us could come up. All the insecurities that we just may *not be good enough* to take this *leap of faith* might be noticeable. All our indifference to even leading a spiritual life could come up. A lot comes up, mostly with an underlying fear that we might be asked to *sacrifice something*. We may feel *pushed* to give up hard-fought ground our ego has taken years to construct through blood, sweat and tears. Being told Christ is here, and also in us, can engender fear—fear gripping our psychic space, that's all. Even if we took no steps to live as the Christ, the fears would still be there. In fact, taking the step to live as the Christ is stepping out of fear altogether. The nature of the Christ Mind is to not justify fear in any way. The Christ is fearless. He spends His day in Love, not fear. But in the presence of the *fearless*, our fear comes up to be released.

> *Nothing real can be threatened.*
> *Nothing unreal exists.*
> *Herein lies the Peace of God.*
>
> *(ACIM; T; Intro)*

Love is a state free of all fears. We only fear when we feel threatened. Most people would agree that a fearless state of being is highly desirable. We don't need a college degree to see fear binds us and sabotages our highest aspirations; Love sets us free and allows us to live up to our highest truth and realizations. Fear makes us depressed; Love brings us unbounded Joy. We are children of Love, not fear. We are beings of Light, not darkness. We are entitled to perfect health and Pure Joy, not meant to be denied these by the results of sickness and sorrow. Embracing Love is nothing short of embracing ourselves as our Divine Creator created us to be.

This is not theory, nor an ideological belief system we project and pursue. We are committed to the removal of "the blocks to the awareness of Love's presence." And Love's presence is Heaven on Earth, not an etheric promise of uncertainty in the afterlife. Nor is it a Utopic projection of some idealized society that *could be.* Life here and now is the domain of Heaven or hell. One can observe quite easily hell. Can we as easily denounce the hell and give energy to the fulfillment of Heaven? Can we be aware of the Love that possesses and governs all things? What would this Heaven state look like, practically speaking, directly and unequivocally in our Life? It is our responsibility in our highest Life purpose to bring the vibrations of Heaven to Earth.

❖

PART 4 is about creating Heaven on Earth. This involves five areas of our Life that work together. Since *the Christ* is the one who fully remembers God, this Heaven-state-of-awareness amounts to:

16. Christ in Ourselves
17. Christ in Our Family
18. Christ in Our Work Place
19. Christ in Our Community
20. Christ in Our Relationship

Christ in ourselves is answering to a higher calling that gives meaning to our Life. Why are we here? What did we come to express? What is our greater purpose? Who are we? We have a direct connection to the Energy that created the whole Cosmos, so what is our awareness of that connection? How attentive are we to our Self-Identity as a Son of God? The Christ is not exclusive to Jesus, although He is the One in charge of the process of Atonement. Complete forgiveness is needed to come into Christ Consciousness. And ultimately this Consciousness is one of *Perfect Happiness*. All errors of misperception are corrected. This is the first step in bringing Heaven to Earth—we must come to the Heaven state within us where all internal conflicts have been brought to a close.

We are at peace with ourselves, and all things around us. This is the beginning of an Inner Peace of Heaven within ourselves.

The second area of *Heaven on Earth* is Christ in our family. We chose this incarnation with those whom we either had some incomplete business or we had signed up ahead of time to help. These are mostly family, relatives, and ancestors who were the main players in our reasons for taking this life. And our parents and siblings, for sure, are our closest people with whom we joined to realize the Christ. Self comes first, then family, relatives and ancestors come next as the main beneficiaries of this action of being our true Self, The Christ. These are the people with whom we must *end the separation*.

Thirdly, much of our life is spent in some kind of work, some kind of endeavor. Those in the workplace are also important to include in this awakening into being the Christ. These are the people with whom we must contend with in the world to be productive—with whom, and perhaps to whom we must have something to give. The people we work with and for are our gurus. They teach us how we are coming across. They receive us mostly as we receive ourselves. These are the teachers and disciples of close quarters. They are beyond the ties of the family, but they are a kind of cast of characters with whom we have bonded and decided something meaningful is to take place. They are our brothers and our keepers. They are the ones we are to help, and from whom we are to receive help. Heaven in the workplace is essential.

Christ in our community could be a conscious or an adjunct result of our right living. Living in the Christ has an all-pervading extension of benefit to the larger community, but we may or may not be consciously responsible and aware of this impact. Look at the hundreds of millions of people Christ has touched since his actual life of 32 or some years as a man in the Middle East two millenniums ago. As the Christ, we may not directly know the effects this will have on our community. This is not our concern. Our concern is the group of people forming our "church," or our tribe of characters woven together in our field of influence. These are the people in our address book, on our Facebook and Twitter, the people who live around us. We are among the ministers of God, and these people are our ministry. We are connected to everyone, past, present, and future, but the community of those around us will automatically derive benefit from these steps we take to realize our true Identity—the Christ.

Last but not least is our partner in life. We join so two may become one—this is a marriage of the *Self on high* with the worldly union of the self of the flesh—or the universal spirit Self with the mind/body self that we brought into this life. It is a Yoga of matrimony. The coming together for the evolution of our souls is clearly an act of being the Christ. We have someone now whose interests are our own, and perhaps even supersede our own. In this Holy Relationship, the opportunity for really giving is demonstrable. It may occur as having children together, having a spiritual mission together, or simply sharing the Joy of one another together. This is what we call, *Spiritual Intimacy*. In the Joy of *Spiritual Intimacy*, both partners awaken in the Christ. We see our partner as the Christ and see ourselves as the Christ. This is the ultimate joining of two souls. This is the ultimate *Heaven on Earth!*

❖

The culmination of the book is discussed in **PART 5**—We Are The Christ. These are the chapters discussed that will take you all the way:

21. Undoing Our Personal Lies
22. Physical Immortality
23. The End of Sickness
24. The Grandeur of Us
25. Constant Happiness

Ultimately in this practice of spiritual awakening, "You are the Christ." My teacher, Tara Singh, would have said, "It is irresponsible not to be the Christ." We can preoccupy ourselves in all kinds of "learning to be" something "better" than we think we are, but all that is a distraction from our true Self-Identity. We are perfectly content "aspiring," yet when it comes to being the Christ, we easily deny, justify not being the Christ, and basically—we chicken out. We are happy to put the Christ up on a pedestal, hanging Him on a cross, put Him in the stained glass scenes in incredible stone structures. But awakening to Him in our heart—that is another matter. Usually, we fall victim to unwillingness. This is the state of affairs in the human psyche—it is unwilling to accept, "We are the Christ."

Why is this? What are the "blocks" to the awareness of Love's presence, and how do we remove them? The main things to remove are negative thoughts, and what we call our "personal lie." The *personal lie* is our most dominant negative judgment about ourselves that is suppressed in our subconscious mind. It's a thought like, "I am not good enough," or "I am not worthy," or "I am always wrong." Thoughts like these are not the real divine truth about us, but part of our mind believes in this unconscious *limitation*. So the first step in *removing the blocks to the awareness of Love's presence* is undoing, or forgiving, the *personal lie*. I devote a whole chapter to this, so don't worry, we can face it and neutralize it together.

Another major block to the *awareness of Love's presence* is our fear—and attraction—to death. Everyone has what we call an *unconscious death urge*. This is a collection of all our negative thoughts and beliefs around death, and our one seemingly insurmountable belief that *death is inevitable*. The unraveling of all these beliefs will lead us to the philosophy and practice of Physical Immortality. A whole chapter is dedicated to this as well. The Christ is immortal, and so are we. Life and death are functions of the Mind. There is no "death" in actuality, but somehow we were conditioned to believe there is. Transition out of the body, which we call "death," is not the end. And, living in the body does not have an inevitable "shelf life." This time here, ultimately dedicated to our Divine Purpose, is totally up to us. We decide when we are born and when we "die" (or *leave the body*). Furthermore, we can stay here in the Physical Universe as long or as short an amount of time that we want to.

The broader implications of Physical Immortality are that we can end all sickness. Sickness is a mistake. It is a defense against the truth. The truth is that God's will for us is perfect happiness and perfect health. Even in the body, perfect health goes hand and hand with a Divine Life. God does not want us to suffer. But we, in our separation from our true *Self*, cause ourselves to suffer (mostly because of suppressed guilt for something). We have to undo the causative thought factors in our mind—our personal beliefs and errors in thought—which are making us *sick!* We can do this. It is not "hard." There is no degree of difficulty in healing ourselves of one thing or another. We can heal cancer as easily as the common cold, says Jesus in *A Course in Miracles*. When our mind-body-spirit are completely integrated (this is the purpose of all Yoga), we will heal ourselves. (You can get our whole book on this subject, *Physical Immortality: How to Overcome Death* at bit.ly/ImmortalRay.)

What do we think will happen when we take full dominion over our mind, over our thoughts, over our bodies, and over our life? We are the co-creators of our happiness, which is already the Will of our Creator for us. Once we get in alignment with that Will, we are harnessing the power that created the Cosmos. This Power is God. This "God" is perfect and whole. It is the Divine Energy the Hawaiians call the "I," coupled with the Divine Father-Mother-Child as One (or Spirit-Mind-Body as One). Every entity in the universe has these four parts to its Self-Identity, and they are naturally integrated and Joyful. A *love of correction* integrates us and puts us in touch with this Self-Identity. It puts us in touch with our Grandeur.

The *Grandeur of Us* is boundless. Infinity itself bows to us—we who are the Christ. We are only potentially aware of this Grandeur in our present state of mind, to a degree. The purpose of this book, *The Second Coming: You Are the Christ,* is to put us in full awareness of Love's presence. We can do this together. In fact, we must do it together. We cannot remove the blocks in us unless we are willing to remove them in another brother or sister. This is a law: "What I give my brother, is my gift to me." (ACIM Lesson # 344) So if we are willing to see the Grandeur in another, guess what ??? –we begin to see it in ourselves as well. Hallelujah!

The Second Coming is a journey we take together. Dear reader, you are my brother. You are my sister. I thank you for reading this far. We will ascend together in the Christ. I guarantee it. Your problems may seem insurmountable, but together we can make it through our blocks to Love. I wrote this book to get both of us to a state of mind in which we can receive constant Joy. The happiness of the Christ is not something that is here today and gone tomorrow; it does not depend on certain conditions to be met, and when they are not met happiness goes out the window. This is not perfect happiness, a state of constant Joy.

Constant Joy is just that—constant. Unbridled Happiness is our birthright. A feeling of well-being is our Divine Inheritance. Our name is God's, and in it, we are united with all living things, and with Him who is our true Self, the Christ. In the Christ—the Divine Creator, Father-Mother-Child as ONE—we join hands and heal the planet and all of the ills we have subjected it to. We ask the Christ to help us in this, and He will. We are united in the Glory of Creation. It is our own Glory and Grandeur. *The Second Coming* is upon us. Expect to be exalted. We are as God created us. We are the Christ. And we deserve *perfect happiness* in this life.

The Second Coming is here and now. It offers *perfect and constant Joy—Pure Joy*. Will we receive it? *A Course in Miracles* is not a mere book. It is a Living Presence of the Christ in our midst. As I often mention in our live seminars, reading *A Course in Miracles* is like sitting in a chair, and across from us in another chair is Jesus sitting, facing us. We are having a transformational conversation with Him. We are asking questions, and He is answering. We are listening, and He is speaking. He is giving us the Word of God. He is giving us the Gifts of God. "Do we want to receive them?" is the only question we need to answer. What do we want to do with our life? The question and the answer are in our hands. *The Second Coming* is here, now, in *A Course in Miracles*. It is in this book as well, which we are holding. I invite you to receive it. Because in the end, you receive your true Self—*You are the Christ.* Are you ready to wake up and receive this great gift today? Why wait? Claim your inheritance now.

Love,

Markus Ray

The Navy Yards
Washington DC.

PART 1

What Is the Christ?

1.
The Mind's Power

When I met Sondra Ray in 1985 she said two things I never forgot: 1) "*A Course in Miracles* is the most important book written in 2000 years." and 2) "Your thought is creative." These may seem overworked declarations after 35 years from the time they were spoken. Self-help gurus have touted the power of the mind ever since then and attempted to channel this power to help an ever self-improving audience to create more successful lifestyles and personal development achievements. Nothing wrong with that, yet those statements sunk deep into my psyche and awakened another potential that was maybe not so concerned with success as measured by my worldly achievements, but certainly moving me toward a life of Constant Happiness and Pure Joy.

I began to immerse myself in *A Course in Miracles*. I had been to college twice and received my Master's Degree in Art, my *MFA*; no professor had ever made such statements like, "This is the most important book written in 2000 years." That had a huge impact on me. What would such a book be, and why was it so important? I began to explore it.

Soon I found out about its origins. It was scribed by a clinical psychologist, Dr. Helen Schucman, in New York City, during the 1960s—70s. But it contained the words of Jesus, the Christ, coming through her, so to speak. And it was not typical of other "channeled" works commonly found in metaphysical bookstores of the day. The scribe was not singing her own praises that such a lofty being had "come through her." In fact, her name was hardly on the book at all. A little reference in the preface to her scribing, but nothing more. The work was set to become the most important book written in 2000 years because it was, in essence, Christ's 2nd Coming which He promised nearly two millennia ago. Here it was, in our very midst. Here it remains, and will remain. Jesus is the author of *A Course in Miracles.*

> *This course has come from him because his words have reached you in a language you can love and understand. Are other teachers possible, to lead the way to those who speak in different tongues and appeal to different symbols? Certainly there are. Would God leave anyone without a very present help in time of trouble; a savior who can symbolize Himself? Yet do we need a many-faceted curriculum, not because of content differences, but because symbols must shift and change to suit the need. Jesus has come to answer yours. In him you find God's Answer. Do you, then, teach with him, for he is with you; he is always here.*
>
> *(ACIM; MT; Section 23; ¶7)*

> ***This is a course in mind training.***
>
> *(ACIM; Text; Chapter 1; Section VII; ¶4)*

Over 1250 pages of "mind training." Why would my mind, after so much compulsory and elective education, need so much training? What was I missing after twelve years of schooling and six years of "higher education" that still required me to somehow retrain my mind? In what was I deficient? What were the levels of understanding I had not yet accessed? Could I say I knew what miracles were, even, least of all claim that I had them? All these questions came to a head and propelled me forward to begin reading *A Course in Miracles*. I could not put it down.

We all want Love in our life. More Love is sought, but like the elusive fish of the ancient Chinese sages, too often escaping from the hook of our cast out fishing lines. What would be needed to hook with certainty the catch of Absolute Love? Absolute Happiness? Absolute Fulfillment? Absolute anything? It seemed to me in 1985 that despite my 18 years of schooling, my world was still lacking the Inner Peace and certainty that would give me what Socrates called *the Good Life*. It seemed like miracles were needed, but what were they? When I opened *A Course in Miracles* and read this, I somehow knew my search was over, and my fishing for the elusive catch of my highest desire would yield actual results:

> *This is a course in miracles. It is a required course. Only the time you take it is voluntary. Free will does not mean that you can establish the curriculum. It means only that you can elect what you want to take at a given time. The course does not aim at teaching the meaning of love, for that is beyond what can be taught. It does aim, however, at removing the blocks to the awareness of love's presence, which is your natural inheritance. The opposite of love is fear, but what is all-encompassing can have no opposite.*
>
> *This course can therefore be summed up very simply in this way:*
>
> ***Nothing real can be threatened.***
> ***Nothing unreal exists.***

(ACIM; Text; Introduction)

I had never read such a thing. What did it mean? It was spoken in words that I clearly understood grammatically, but what was the nature of this curriculum? It said it is a "required course." It referred to my *free will,* and the extent of what I could determine, and what I could not determine. It said I could not determine the content of this *Course*, but I could decide to take it or not, and I could determine when I would take it. That was the extent of my *free will.* It could be now, later, or never. Then it said something interesting about love. It referred to love as something *beyond what can be taught*, something that is our natural inheritance. Here is stated the purpose of the *Course*: it aims to *remove the blocks to the awareness of love's presence.* Put all together—it is a mind training to remove the misperceptions in my mind to the awareness of love.

The Mind has a Power that it is accessible, but I am blocking this Power with fear. I sometimes feel threatened in life. To feel threatened is to feel fear, yes? And this introduction tells me that "Nothing real can be threatened." This Power could be called the *real.* The real could be called Love. Love cannot be threatened, at least the Love that is real. What comes to mind is Shakespeare's statement, "Love is not love which alters, when alteration finds." Love does not change in the face of change. Love is constant, unchanging, not able to be *threatened.* It is a presence, and this presence is all-pervasive, but my awareness of it can be blocked. The miracle uses this Power to remove the blocks.

The Mind has a Power. It is aware of the *real* and cannot be fooled by the *threatenable*—the *unreal.* It dismisses the unreal for the awareness of the real. This Power is fully operational in the Christ. He or she who has taken up this book to awaken themselves has access to this Power of the Mind. Christ's Mind is on every page of *A Course in Miracles*, ready to "remove the blocks to the awareness of love's presence." In this removal is the *miracle.*

Miracles are transformations out of fear into love. This is the basis of the whole *Course.* As we read on in the Text, Jesus makes the Power of the Mind very clear. The Mind is always creating something, and we have a choice of what we will create with this Power.

> *Few appreciate the real power of the mind, and no one remains fully aware of it all the time. However, if you hope to spare yourself from fear there are some things you must realize, and realize fully. The mind is very powerful, and never loses its creative force. It never sleeps. Every instant it is creating. It is hard to recognize that thought and belief combine into a power surge that can literally move mountains. It appears at first glance that to believe such power about yourself is arrogant, but that is not the real reason you do not believe it. You prefer to believe that your thoughts cannot exert real influence because you are actually afraid of them. This may allay awareness of the guilt, but at the cost of perceiving the mind as impotent. If you believe that what you think is ineffectual you may cease to be afraid of it, but you are hardly likely to respect it. There are no idle thoughts. All thinking produces form at some level.*
>
> *(ACIM; Text; Chapter 2; Section VI; ¶ 9)*

How can we read this passage and not be totally committed to *mind training?* This passage reaffirmed in me the truth of what Sondra Ray had said: *thought is always creative.* "The mind never loses its creative force. It never sleeps." Even in your dreams, it is creating. "There are no idle thoughts. All thinking produces form at some level." The Power of the mind is in us whether we are aware of it or not. It is an essential part of the Christ. He is one in touch with the Power of His mind, and He uses it to express the *real*, the unthreatenable Love that created Him.

But are we afraid of this Power, using the excuse that it is "arrogant" to believe we have such Power. Power is Energy. It is an Energy that can "move mountains." It is hard to believe in this Power completely, especially that we have access to it. But later in the Lessons, we are assured that when our will is consistent with the will of our Creator, we are given all the Power we need to do anything:

My Father gives all power unto me.

The Son of God is limitless. There are no limits on his strength, his peace, his joy, nor any attributes his Father gave in his creation. What he wills with his Creator and Redeemer must be done. His holy will can never be denied, because his Father shines upon his mind, and lays before it all the strength and love in earth and Heaven. I am he to whom all this is given. I am he in whom the power of my Father's Will abides.

Your Will can do all things in me, and then extend to all the world as well through me. There is no limit on Your Will. And so all power has been given to Your Son.

(ACIM; Workbook; Lesson #320)

Now, we must understand in the Lessons of *ACIM* that when we are addressed directly, they really mean it. When the lesson says, "My Father gives all power unto me," that means you and me! Who else is in the room?

We have to get the order right here and understand Jesus is talking to us. These are statements given to us to lift us into higher consciousness, free of limitations. This consciousness is the Christ Mind, or Christ's Vision, and Jesus is here in His first-person Voice to lead us there. When the Lesson says, "I am he to whom all this is given. I am he in whom the power of my Father's Will abides," that means you and me very specifically. When the "Son of God" is mentioned, this means you and me as well. The notion that Jesus is the "only Son of God," and we are not "sons and daughters" of God is corrected in no uncertain terms. Who do you think created you? God, the Father/Mother would not deny this Power of life to any part of creation. Therefore, all this Power, given through God to the Son, is yours and mine:

> *It should especially be noted that God has only one Son. If all His creations are His Sons, everyone must be an integral part of the whole Sonship. The Sonship in its Oneness transcends the sum of its parts. However, this is obscured as long as any of its parts is missing. That is why the conflict cannot ultimately be resolved until all the parts of the Sonship have returned. Only then can the meaning of wholeness in the true sense be understood. Any part of the Sonship can believe in error or incompleteness if he so chooses. However, if he does so, he is believing in the existence of nothingness. The correction of this error is the Atonement.*
>
> *(ACIM; Text; Chapter 2; Section VII; ¶ 6)*

Oneness does transcend the sum of its parts, but each "part" is essential to the ultimate unification, or Atonement—"at-one-ment." Oneness includes not only us but every other human being on the planet—past, present and future. *E Plurbus Unum,* scribed on the Great Seal of the United States, is in keeping with this unification—"one out of many." There is only the One, composed in the plurality of all its essential parts.

The Power of the Mind to create is based on the absolute knowledge of this Oneness. Other conditions are implied. He Who is One would not do anything that would limit or take away from another part. He would not kill or steal from, or banish from his sphere of influence any other member of the Sonship. He would place in quarantine anyone infectious, with the strong expectation of that person's healing and return. His personal preferences become secondary to the Good of the Whole. His actions are based on the Good of the Whole. He gives peace and joy to all; He gives compassion and forgiveness to all; He gives non-judgment to all; He suspends any anger and conflict and lives in the inner calm of real Power. Peace is Power. This is the Power of the Mind in the realization of the Christ in you and me.

2. The Known Is Past

We are taught as children that education and knowledge form the doorway to the good life. In a worldly sense, the broader our knowledge on any subject makes us more effective and expert in that subject. Yet, can the more important qualities in life—love, liberty, and the pursuit of happiness—be acquired through the channels of how much we know? The accumulations of knowledge have not solved the problems of human life. Certainly, we have invented all kinds of technological wonders that are useful. Yet, we have within this field of the known memories of tremendous suffering, pain, and despair. Has the known liberated us from these negative experiences? Probably not. Memory keeps them alive, and we tend to repeat them over and over with slightly different players and circumstances.

What is the nature of the known? What is knowledge? Krishnamurti describes knowledge as the "accumulation of memory." In other words, all that the human race has experienced, collected and learned, put together in the conglomerate of memory, of all past thought, forms the basis of knowledge. This *field of the known* contains all the thoughts of the sciences, politics, religions, psychologies, emotional tendencies, family patterns and ancestries, personal preferences, and virtually everything that the human race has experienced in its past time and life on earth. Yet, this knowledge is partial, not complete, and therefore divided and in conflict with itself. Therefore, the nature of knowledge is to be incomplete perennially. What is incomplete has tension and conflict. Intrinsically within the field of the known is conflict. And where there is conflict, there cannot be freedom, love, and happiness, in the true sense of these states of being. Conflict and love are mutually exclusive. Therefore, love does not exist in the field of the known. Substitutes for love, such as attachment and pleasure exist in the known, but these are relative, not absolute. They can shift and change in time to their opposites, Therefore, they are not eternally in the present. And only the eternal merits the name of Love, Truth, Freedom, Happiness, Peace, Joy, etc.

Jesus tells us early on in *ACIM* not to trust thought and the meaning we ascribe to things. "My thoughts do not mean anything." (Lesson #10) "I have given everything I see all the meaning it has for me." (Lesson #2) "I do not understand anything I see." (Lesson #3) "I see only the past." (Lesson #7) "I see nothing as it is now." (Lesson #9) "My meaningless thoughts are showing me a meaningless world." (Lesson #11) "I am upset because I see a meaningless world." (Lesson #12) Where does this leave us in life? We are operating with a thought system, "the known," that is incomplete, in constant conflict and uncertainty, mostly composed of images from the past—essentially illusions. And this view of life based on what we "know," which is very limited, is extremely upsetting. This view "engenders fear," He says. (Lesson #13) It is not the domain of what we are seeking: Love, Peace, and Joy.

Why is the past so unreliable? To a great degree, we need memory. We need the past. We need to learn how to drive a car. Without memory we could not communicate with language—I could not write these words to you, my readers, without my past knowledge of English. Even finding our house at our address is a function of memory; catching our plane at the right time requires thought. Functioning in the material world is a function of thought and memory, which is of the past. We need it. Yet, in the realm of the absolute, we need to rise above the past and place our awareness on the all-pervasive present. This awareness transcends thought.

We are so much in the momentum of thought, it requires great attention to step out of its habit, and still the mind of all its incessant "chatter." Meditation is the observation of this dynamic of thought, a turning inward to place attention on the content of the mind. In so doing there is a slowing down of this momentum. The space between thoughts becomes wider until one's attention rests more on the space of emptiness than on the thoughts themselves. In this slowing down of thought, the senses are heightened in their contact with the present. Interpretive "thinking" comes to a stop, and there is a peace in the present which sees without judgments and motivations. One enters a state of mind that is still and empty. One enters a dimension of time that is only in the present.

Preoccupied with the past, the mind seeks familiarity, even if that past was painful and full of fear and problems. Yet the mind always has a choice in this matter. Will it "think" the thoughts of the past (the ego of me and mine) or the Thoughts of God in the present (the Holy Spirit and the Christ Mind)?

> *The one wholly true thought one can hold about the past is that it is not here. To think about it at all is therefore to think about illusions. Very few have realized what is actually entailed in picturing the past or in anticipating the future. The mind is actually blank when it does this, because it is not really thinking about anything.*
>
> *(ACIM; Workbook; Lesson #8)*

There you have it. Thoughts of the past are images that are not really here. Freedom from the known is freedom from the past. Most of what we "know" is from the past. Most of what we anticipate for the future is based on the past as well. We are stuck in the confines of memory which keep us bound to old experiences, which have already passed and are no longer fully relevant. The mind has a greater potential than to stay stuck in the illusions of the past. When we see that the past is a limitation, we begin to question ourselves and ask if it is possible to be free of this tendency to rehash what has already gone by.

> ***The past is over. It can touch me not.***
>
> *Unless the past is over in my mind, the real world must escape my sight. For I am really looking nowhere; seeing but what is not there. How can I then perceive the world forgiveness offers? This the past was made to hide, for this the world that can be looked on only now. It has no past. For what can be forgiven but the past, and if it is forgiven it is gone.*
>
> *Father, let me not look upon a past that is not there. For You have offered me Your Own replacement, in a present world the past has left untouched and free of sin. Here is the end of guilt. And here am I made ready for Your final step. Shall I demand that You wait longer for Your Son to find the loveliness You planned to be the end of all his dreams and all his pain?*
>
> *(ACIM; Workbook; Lesson #289)*

The *real world* is defined in *A Course in Miracles* as a place of Pure Joy. It is a heaven on earth. You may say that this is not possible to have, but then you would be invalidating the Power of the Mind to determine its fate, to create its Divine Reality, as discussed in Chapter 1.

The real world shows a world seen differently, through quiet eyes and with a mind at peace. Nothing but rest is there. There are no cries of pain and sorrow heard, for nothing there remains outside forgiveness. And the sights are gentle. Only happy sights and sounds can reach the mind that has forgiven itself.

(ACIM; Workbook; Preamble to Lessons #291-#300)

What are the benefits of being free of the past? Admittedly, the memory of the past is needed for daily bodily and worldly functions, yet the purpose of existence is not just the mere survival of our ego's version of life. The purpose of existence is to transcend the dualities of thought and to be in the Presence of a Unified Field of Joy. This perfect happiness is akin to God, and this awareness is our birthright to achieve. You could say our purpose here on earth is to be free of pain, sorrow and death, and to live a Life Immortal in the vibrations of Infinite Intelligence. And—we cannot do this as long as we are clinging to the small bit of the *known* we have accumulated. We must go beyond the limitations of thought and step into the vastness of the Unknown, the timeless and the all-pervasive. We have to have a relationship with the present and be liberated from the guilt of the past and fear of the future. This is obvious.

How does one free himself from the past if mistakes were made? The memory of these mistakes is often tainting our life in the present. We may be carrying huge amounts of regret and guilt. How does one deal with these emotional sabotages of our present? Yes, the past is over, but the memory of these negative events are still very much alive in our minds. How do we overcome this memory? We have invented whole fields of psychology to address Post Traumatic Syndrome Disorders, PTSD, but what would actually get people over the memories of past stress and despair? Rehashing over the past does not free us from it. Analyzing garbage does not get rid of the crud.

"Forgiveness is the key to happiness." This is Lesson #121 in *A Course in Miracles'* Workbook. How do we best apply this key to enter through the doorway of our eternal innocence? Here again, it is important to distinguish between the "mind of thought" (the past, the ego, the limitations of memory) and the "Mind of God" (the present, the true Self, the boundlessness of our real Mind of the Spirit we all share). In the mind of memory, the events of the past seem very "real." There may be past actions for which we may still need to make amends or pay back some debt. We are always able to do this. Perhaps physically this is not possible, but psychically it is always possible. But we also have to see that in the Mind of God, our true Self, the infractions we thought we did or thought someone else did to us, did not even occur. This is a very high perspective. Many will ask, "How can you say the Holocaust did not occur?" Well, on the level of bodies and personal egos, it did occur. And this is lamentable. But Spiritual vision is asking us to rise above this level of the body and see the level of Spirit, true Identity, in which "death of the body" does not affect the immortal life of the Spirit. At the level of an immortal life of the Spirit, these horrible events "did not occur." In the sense, they had no real consequences to the Self Identities of all parties involved, from both sides of perpetrators and victims.

This kind of vision is free of the past. It is free of the known. It is free of the pain and suffering stored in the memory of the mind/body. It is free of the judgments of future generations. And it is this vision that has its positive effects on the mind/body. The mind (of God) connected with its innocence is a competant director of the body, and all of its various functions, including its health. A mind that thinks thoughts of innocence and joy is far more beneficial to the health of the body than a mind that is preoccupied with past hurts, mistakes, and infractions. A mind willing to forgive and let go is far more a healing factor of bodily disease than a mind holding on to hate and grievances. Forgiveness is the key to entering this mind of innocence because the past is transmuted to a neutral memory that does not have the negative charge of guilt or blame. In the vibration of innocence, the past is rendered benign, the present is imbued with Pure Joy, and the future is expected to be different than the past in its unfolding of the Pure Joy of the present.

3. Freedom Is Present

The Cosmic Forces of Creation are unconditionally and absolutely free, and always present for us to tap into them. Divine Laws of Love imbue every atom in all space and time with a giving of Life beyond measure. This giving is in the present and extends itself into infinity. This giving is immensely joyful. This giving is embodied in you and me. We live by these Cosmic Forces in us. By these Cosmic Forces, we are unconditionally and absolutely free as well.

We may think governments bestow us with freedom. The power of those at the top of imperial and political governing bodies of dominance would have us think that our freedom comes from the orders and rules they establish, oversee and provide. Law and order functions on the assumptions that 1) all governments' rules made are for the good of the whole of society 2) justice prevails in the system that implements these rules.

We would all agree that traffic lights at an intersection prevent car crashes from happening. We would all agree that laws that prohibit stealing from your neighbor are for the good of all concerned. But the inequities of socio and economic backgrounds amidst people make it almost impossible for us to say that governments bestow freedom. They try from the basis of thought to bring some balance to the social fabric, but as we saw in the last chapter thought falls vastly short of absolute states of Truth, Simplicity, and Love that would truly make us equal and free. People come forth from the family consciousness they were born into, and these have a huge impact on their awareness of higher states of being. One born into poverty may have less opportunity than one born into affluence to receive the adequate preparations to free their minds from sorrow, survival, and the bondage of the past. Yet, someone from humble means may also be more questioning of the systems that keep us bound to our backgrounds and history.

What does it mean to be absolutely and unconditionally free? How would a person experience this state of being? Everything in life has its own nature, its own intrinsic qualities. This nature can be stifled, but not altered in its original character. Water that is dammed up still has its intrinsic tendency to flow downhill. A bird in a cage will still fly when released from the cage. Our eyes in a totally dark room will still see the resplendent colors when taken into the glory of mid-day. The soul of humankind still seeks its most unfettered conditions of freedom no matter how bound it may be to the conditions of its circumstances of survival.

Father, my freedom is in You alone.
(ACIM; Workbook; Lesson #321)

This statement is unequivocal and absolute. "Alone" means "only." *Father* is the Cosmic Force of creation. It is the Life Force that flows through everything. Always present, this Force provides our freedom. We always have it. It is vast and unlimited. Where does the Cosmos end? We cannot say. We do not know. The "Father" is reflected in the known but is vastly present in the Unknown, beyond our thought and comprehension. Freedom is the same. We experience Freedom on different levels. Mostly as cognitive beings, we have absolute freedom of the Mind. We can rule our Mind, and this is the basis for free will. We can think the thoughts we choose to think about. We can think the lower thoughts of the ego which are always limited in some way, and bound to conditions; or we can use the Mind of God, the Father, to take us into higher realms of freedom. We have free will to do this, but we would have to see beyond the limitations of the past and the "known" stored in our conditioning.

What is the original nature of being human? Many saints and philosophers mention free will as the aspect of human beings that set them apart from the other forms of life. We have free will to say "no" to our intrinsic nature, and cause ourselves to suffer. We have free will to "kill." We have free will to deny the existence of "God," a benevolent Life Force that created us and is conducive to our well-being. We have free will to postpone our awakening to Love. We have free will to change our minds as well. What is freedom?

The Dictionary defines it thus:

freedom | ˈfrē dəm | noun

1. The power or right to act, speak, or think as one wants without hindrance or restraint: *we do have some freedom of choice | he talks of revoking some of the freedoms.*
2. Absence of subjection to foreign domination or despotic government: *he was a champion of Irish freedom.*
3. The state of not being imprisoned or enslaved: *the shark thrashed its way to freedom.*
4. The state of being physically unrestricted and able to move easily: *the shorts have a side split for freedom of movement.*

> 5. (Freedom from) the state of not be subject to or affected by (a particular undesirable thing): *government policies to achieve freedom from want.*
> 6. The power of self-determination attributed to the will; the quality of being independent of fate or necessity: *he searched his soul to act from the freedom of his inner convictions.*
> 7. Unrestricted use of something: *the dog is happy having the freedom of the house when we are out.*
> *8*. Familiarity or openness in speech or behavior: *freedom of the press prevailed in an otherwise hostile environment.*

Freedom is the power to act according to the inner convictions of one's own will, unrestrained nor enslaved by the domination or control of an external governing body or ideology. Yet, one could say despotic rulers who inflict great harm on other groups of humanity with their political and military power are acting from a kind of "freedom." Napoleon swept *freely* across Europe devastating much in his path toward world domination and control. However, we must reach for a higher understanding and definition of freedom.

Divine freedom is void of suffering and violence. To exercise true freedom does not take away the freedom of others. What is divinely free is free for all beings. Therefore, people who seek to subjugate or extinguish whole other races or groups of people are not acting from this intrinsic and true freedom. Quite the contrary, they are acting from fear, anger, domination, and control—asserting their will over the lives of others to glorify their ego. Kings, rulers and politicians have done this since time immemorial. Despotic rulers of the more violent tribes seek dominance over other less defended and peaceful tribes. This can happen on a national and cultural scale, as we have seen over and over in the course of human history, filled with the likes of Caesar, Genghis Khan, Napoleon, Hitler, and various domineering economic and military empires.

What we may have called freedom is not real freedom. This is why Jesus has to say:

Father, my freedom is in You alone.
(ACIM; Workbook; Lesson #321)

Divine freedom, bestowed on us by our Creator (which is bestowed equally on every living particle and wave in creation) is the only real freedom. Therefore, all the other freedoms that come down from the edicts of the constitutional halls and bodies of government are lesser than, and even indicative of this greater Universal Freedom. To surrender to the Freedom of Love is the only real surrender, in the end. Can we do it? This has been the perennial question of the saints, gurus, and philosophers from time immemorial.

What does this Divine Connection feel like? How would our lives be changed in the vibration of this Absolute Freedom? Can we drop all notions and pursuits we sought to bring us more happiness and freedom, which only ended in more pressure and bondage? Many are convinced that economic freedom is the main goal in life and that a big bank account gives one more power and freedom. Affluence does give a person more options in the world, and more facility to move around and make more choices. It does allow one to have things of excellence and beauty. It does appear to instill more spaciousness and generosity. But beyond the basic needs and necessities of one's own Life Mission and makeup, does economic surplus grant this Divine Freedom? It may enhance one's direction toward it, but the Source of Divine Freedom cannot be purchased with money in the end. It takes a conviction to relinquish all those things one sought, which fell short of taking a person all the way to complete and total Liberation of his or her Soul.

If I am bound my Father is not free.
(ACIM; Workbook; Lesson #278)

The bindings of the conflicts of thought prevent us from realizing our complete freedom, but furthermore, these are also a restraint placed on our Creator. As we tend to ascribe to our Creator the shortcomings in ourselves, this lack of freedom manifests in the notion of a punishing God who metes out damnation to the sinners under His final judgment. Not only has thought bound us to conditions of fear, conflict, and suffering, but it has bound our Creator to conditions in which the help we could receive from the Cosmic Life Force is unavailable to help us.

Yet, fortunately to us, this limitation only exists in the illusion of our thought. In reality, there is Freedom that is unaffected by the bindings of human judgments:

Creation's freedom promises my own.
(ACIM; Workbook; Lesson #279)

This inherent freedom in Creation assures us that we will find and realize our own. It is a "promise," which means it is inevitable. A promise must be kept by the Cosmic Forces of Life to help us be free. The inherent part of our being is already free, consistent with these forces. We need only make contact with this inherent part of our being.

Within the field of the known, there is fear. Fear binds us and keeps us from freedom. Fear is concerned with the past, projected onto the present and the future. Is it possible for us to transcend fear? Over and over there are references in *A Course in Miracles* that there are only two emotions from which all others stem: Love or fear. There are also statements that *deny* the reality of fear. "Fear is never justified." is Lesson #240. "There is nothing to fear." is Lesson #48. Our preoccupations with traumas from the past keep us in fear, yet the past is over, not here and now. To be truly free we must transcend fear and be in the energy of the present. This is where true freedom is realized.

We are as God created us. We are unequivocally free already, except for our incarcerations of thought. We have dominion over our mind, and therefore we can step out of the conditions of thought that keep us bound. In this present freedom, there is great Joy and Happiness. Why would we wish to remain bound when we can step out of the confines of thought?

My present happiness is all I see.
(ACIM; Workbook; Lesson #290)

Freedom and happiness go together. One cannot be bound and be happy. One cannot be unequivocally free and not experience Pure Joy.

Freedom is present. Are we there to meet it? My teacher Tara Singh said, "Peace is always present, but we are absent." That means that we are preoccupied with past thoughts that keep us distracted from the reality of the present. Therefore, we are not with the Peace that exists only in the present. The same applies to any absolute quality. Freedom is present, not in the future or the past. It is a quality of now. And in this *now*, there are no other conditions that distract us. We are either with it or not. We are either free or not. And this freedom is available to us now. No matter what other conditions seem to prevent or block us from an awareness of this present, they cannot keep us from making contact with our inherent reality. Even death can be overcome in this inherent state of freedom:

There is no death. The Son of God is free.

Death is a thought that takes on many forms, often unrecognized. It may appear as sadness, fear, anxiety or doubt; as anger, faithlessness and lack of trust; concern for bodies, envy, and all forms in which the wish to be as you are not may come to tempt you. All such thoughts are but reflections of the worshipping of death as savior and as giver of release.

God made not death. Whatever form it takes must therefore be illusion. This the stand we take today. And it is given us to look past death, and see the life beyond.

(ACIM; Workbook; Lesson #163)

The freedom in the present is bestowed by God Who created us. It is the Life Force itself that has no opposite. It is free of all negativity, all suffering, all pain, all sorrow. It is the Force which makes the planets spin. The movement of the stars. The beating of the heart. The inflow and outflow of breath. It is forever in the present for our benefit. It is the very nature of our holy Self, Who is the ruler of our highest destiny of Eternal Life and unlimited Joy!

4.
Christ Is the Link

Never in my lifetime has the Christ been so well explained as by my teacher, Tara Singh, in a four-part commentary he gave on this subject titled "What is the Christ?" The deeper meaning of the preamble to Lessons #271-280 is discussed, as well as his very confronting questions as to why we have not accepted ourselves as God created us. Taraji points out the irresponsibility of our egos, by which we live, which deny we are the Christ and make up a personality in which our problems reign. When I heard this lecture my whole world was turned upside down. I had to face the fact that it was my own choice *not to be the Christ*, my Higher Self. And seeing this, what was I going to do about it? It was a sober moment, as often were the moments of acute awareness that Tara Singh brought other students and me to face in ourselves.

The preamble to Lessons #271-280 is titled, "What is the Christ." It begins with this definition, which brings more clarity to this subject than I had ever heard:

> *Christ is God's Son, as He created Him. He is the Self we share, uniting us with one another, and with God Himself.*
>
> *(ACIM; Workbook; Preamble to Lessons #271-280)*

These statements have tremendous implications. They correct so much of the false theology that was fed to us as children, especially the notion that Jesus is the "only Son of God," and that we are "sinners." They also make it clear that Christ is not a separate entity outside of ourselves. Rather, "He is the Self we share." And in this sharing of a common Self, we are united with each other. Furthermore, this Christ Self is the link we have with our Creator as well. We are connected to God through the Christ. Awareness of this Self is the primary goal in Life, which is to be aware of our true Identity in God.

You may say "I am Joe, or Mary, or Sam, but not the Christ." OK. We all have a personality we made up in the world, but this does not exclude the more subtle Self who we did not *make up*. This Self we share is God created, not made up by the ego as a *separated* entity. Ascending our own ladder of holiness, it is essential we accept and forgive the *self we made up* to have contact with the Self Whom God created. We made a huge mistake in thinking we were separate from this Self, but it can be corrected. And this correction sees no *sin*. There is nothing for which to be judged or condemned; in fact, that is only the tendency of the ego—the self we made up—to judge and condemn. The Christ condemns nothing; He looks upon the devastation our egos have made of Life, forgives it, and restores our minds to their original Self-Identity of Peace and Joy.

What could be better? One would think this awareness would instigate an immediate transformation. Yet, there is one more major factor we need to face in this transition from the ego-self we made up to the Christ Self which God created—and this is *inherent unwillingness*. Tara Singh made this remarkably clear. The reason we do not step into our true

Self, which could be as easy as passing through a doorway, is that the mind by which we think—the ego's mind we made up with all of its knowledge and accumulated memory—is inherently unwilling to pass through this door. It sees it as a death, which it would be, to avoid at all costs, even if this resistance brings more suffering and death of the body/mind closer to us. We are unwilling to be the Christ. We are perfectly willing to be the ego with all of its problems, confusion, conflicts, and dilemmas. But to step into our real Self of the Christ, we have tremendous resistance.

Now, how do we deal with unwillingness? First, see the fact that we have it. It manifests as the perennial conflict in the human condition, in our condition. We know it is good to love our neighbor, but we cannot seem to give up our blame and grievances toward him. We know it is good to love our self, but we cannot seem to be free of our self-judgments and incomplete concerns and inner conflicts. This is the nature of unwillingness: *I want more love*, yet, *I do not want more love if it means I have to change and correct myself.* Inner correction is the only way out of this quagmire of unwillingness. We need to experience the Peace and Joy that ensues from inner correction, and not be afraid of it. Only the ego can feel humiliated or uncomfortable when it sees a mistake that requires correction. We must pass through these states of discomfort with a determination to deal with this basic issue of unwillingness.

I am determined to see things differently.
(ACIM; Workbook; Lesson #21)

There may be no means to overcome a tendency, in the sense that any means we use would be born of the tendency itself. The ego cannot undo the ego; unwillingness cannot overcome unwillingness. So what can free us from unwillingness? We have to go "outside the system" of thought. Determination is something more rarified than thought. It sees the limitations of the "known;" it sees the attempts to rise up in holiness are often thwarted by ego tendencies that sabotage this ascension; it sees that our best interests are not always served by our methods; it sees that the past is strong in its hold on our memories; determination sees that the solutions must come from a different "unknown" space than from the mind that made the problem itself. Determination is a kind of surrender to a *Higher Power*. When all else fails, which is the nature of unwillingness, we have access to this Higher Power that can breakthrough. The Christ Mind is in touch with this determination. The Christ Mind is the link that we all share to rise into the potentials of our true Identity, where the real solutions lie.

We heal through grace and the boundless mercy of our Creator. It is not through efforts. Yet, it is through our attention paid to this force of inner correction which *rights the wrongs* of our misperceptions and unwillingness. Through grace, we are taken to heights of awareness that we would not otherwise be able to reach. Mercy is the action of healing and holiness that comes to us even though we may not be ready or able to receive it.

God in His mercy, wills that I be saved.
(ACIM; Workbook; Lesson #235)

Mercy implies forgiveness, and absolution rendered for a mistake that may otherwise call for punishment. The forgiveness of illusions we have previously maintained is the action of God's mercy. In this action is implied that illusions have no real consequences because what is not real can have no real effects. And this is why total forgiveness is always justified. It is the epitome of Divine Mercy. Christ is the person whose Mind is permeated with absolute Mercy and Grace, through complete forgiveness, which He gives freely to all those He touches and meets.

It is through Mercy and Grace that we will overcome our unwillingness to change. These are actions of the Divine Itself. They are activated only when we stop projecting our own "means for salvation." We have to come empty-handed to the Christ Mind within us to have this kind of help, but otherwise, we are stuck in the grip of unwillingness. What do we have to lose? All the former means we have employed to free ourselves from our limitations have more or less stopped short of total liberation. We are linked to the Christ by the very nature of our Being, so why not tap into the Power of His healing benevolence within us to rise to the truth of who we are? We can pass through the door to our true Self when we go empty-handed without any other expectations or agenda. In this emptiness resides the Power of the Christ to save us from the hell of unwillingness.

Christ is not an external personage or a holy entity outside of our Self. *He is the Self we share.* Christ is the link between us, between us and God, between us and our higher Identity, between us and our greatest potential to manifest our heaven on earth. The "second coming" of the Christ is merely the awareness that you are the Christ. You and I are the Christ in our Highest potential of the Self we share. This may seem like arrogance, but is it arrogance to accept ourselves as God created us? Or is it arrogance to "deny what God created" by insisting on a substitute *self we made up* to usurp the role of our true Self-Identity? This is the real arrogance of the ego to make up a false self, even one that has the semblance of holiness—by insisting that it is a "sinner" in need of salvation from a made-up "Christ" Who "died for our sins."

It is the resurrection that established the Christ as the Christ, not the crucifixion. The fact that He forgave everyone and rose up beyond the consequences of "death" proved that He was the Christ Immortal. He asserted there is no death. Only Life is real, and only total forgiveness is justified in a world gone crazy with hate and attack, guilt and punishment. Christ is the link to the innocence that is inherent in our Being.

Within the advent of our own awakening into this Christ Mind, we too can accept our innocence and be absolved of all guilt we may be carrying from our past, right in this holy instant.

This holy instant is the boon of the Christ to free us from the hell of guilt we made. And this holy instant is right here and right now. Any mistake from our past can be corrected and its "consequences" rendered null and void from the holy instant of linking up with the Christ in us. When will we accept this truth of our Mind as the governing guide in our life? It is available. We have to make this one decision to accept it. We have to link up with the Christ in our mind, beyond the limitations of thought. But we probably will resist and postpone this decision. It is too easy. Or it is too threatening to our egos that are addicted to thought and all of its struggles.

5.
Total Forgiveness

The purpose of life is to be free of all problems, sorrow, pain, suffering and even death, and to make contact with our Self-Identity as God created us. We are linked to the Christ Self who makes manifest this state of being. Our job is to be more and more in the vibration of this Self-Identity, which means to discover the Christ at the base of our being, not just as a religious concept we were conditioned to believe in as children. *The Christ* is not a personality, or even exclusively referring to Jesus. The Christ is a state of being in which the universal Self is reached, in contact with and extending forth unconditional Love which is the nature of the Cosmos.

When this contact is established, Pure Joy is felt. It is extended in all of our actions, and our expressions in Life become songs of Truth, Simplicity, Love, and Service. In this state of being it does not matter so much "what we do" as much as the quality of how we do it. Are we infused with the Love of God? Love of our Brothers and Sisters? Does this Love come through our actions? These are our primary Life questions.

OK. Most of us would say we are not there yet. We may not honestly say we are the Christ, our Higher Self; nor can we say that it is not possible to be that. What would get us there? What is the most important action of the Christ? What is the most important action in our life?

Forgiveness is the key to happiness.
(ACIM; Workbook; Lesson #121)

What is this key of which Jesus speaks? We may have notions of forgiveness that are not what He is talking about. We must see forgiveness in the light of truth. The world's version usually looks something like this: "You did some dastardly deed from which I am adversely affected; because I am holier than thou, I let you off the hook even though you don't deserve it." In this version, people naturally have an aversion to even the word forgiveness, because they perceive themselves pardoning something in another that is "unpardonable." In other words, the other party is still guilty as hell. "But I will prove I am so far above the situation with my acts of mercy, so others see I am better than the person who perpetrated the wrongdoing."

This is not the version of forgiveness that Jesus puts forth in *A Course in Miracles*. His version takes into account different levels of being. He is already resurrected into the higher level of being, beyond thought and beyond the body, so He stays in a state unthreatenable by anything. He is not at all affected by the externals and coming from the basis of the internal, He is in a state of perfect peace all of the time. From this higher vantage point, forgiveness looks like this:

> *The strength of pardon is its honesty, which is so uncorrupted that it sees illusions as illusions, not as truth. It is because of this that it becomes the undeceiver in the face of lies; the great restorer of the simple truth. By its ability to overlook what is not there, it opens up the way to truth, which has*

been blocked by dreams of guilt. Now are you free to follow in the way your true forgiveness opens up to you. For if one brother has received this gift of you, the door is open to yourself.

There is a simple way to find the door to true forgiveness, and perceive that it is open wide in welcome. When you feel that you are tempted to accuse someone of sin in any form, do not allow your mind to dwell on what you think he did, for that is self-deception. Ask instead, "Would I accuse myself of doing this"?

(ACIM; Workbook; Lesson #134)

It's a bit reminiscent of His statements in the Bible when He confronted the men who wanted to stone the prostitute: "He who is free of all wrongdoing cast the first stone." Well, none of them were, so none could throw that first rock of guilt.

But the other important factor here is about the levels—the level of truth and the level of illusion. This is hard for people to get. At the level of the personality self we made up, shit happens. Things go wrong, and people do things we don't like. And even we make mistakes we regret. Here is where the glitch is. We give great meaning to this level of existence, and it may not even be the highest form of existence we can muster up. Jesus in *A Course in Miracles* would go so far to say it is meaningless because it is separated from our Divine Being which is our natural state of Pure Joy. We are most of the time not even in our True Self. Much of science would deny there even is such a thing. Only mystics, certain philosophers, and holy men and women from time immemorial have made contact with it. But this is our only real goal in life—to attain the heaven state on earth—the awareness of our well-being and happiness all of the time. More and more we are beginning to see this is a strictly internal matter. Our mental states and internal vibrations result in what we see and experience in the *external world.* Shit, in other words, does not *just happen*; we bring it upon ourselves with our vibrational field for some lessons to be learned.

The level of Truth according to *A Course in Miracles* is that you are Spirit, and this state of being is perfectly invulnerable to attack of any kind. It cannot be burnt, drowned, shot, whipped, crucified or killed. It is your Immortal Being that always was and always will be. At this level of being, the infractions you believed another perpetrated upon you, or you upon another, never even occurred. "What!" you will say. "What about someone killed in a car accident by a drunk driver? What about a murder *victim?* And what about whole groups of people killed in wars and acts of genocide? Are you going to say this did not occur?" Well, yes, at the Spirit level this did not occur. Leaving this body does not affect the Self-Identity of the Spirit. But we think that it does, and that is why we need the process of forgiveness to get out of our angst and upset.

> *Forgiveness recognizes what you thought your brother did to you has not occurred. It does not pardon sins and make them real. It sees there was no sin. And in that view are all your sins forgiven. What is sin, except a false idea about God's Son? Forgiveness merely sees its falsity, and therefore lets it go. What then is free to take its place is now the Will of God.*
>
> *(ACIM; Workbook; Preamble to Lessons 221-230)*

This is going to plug-in a lot of people who want to hang on to their victimhood, and blame others for the downside of their fate. Some will not agree that there is no sin; in fact, the whole Catholic Church is based on the belief in "original sin." Or, at the least, there is a feeling that circumstances "beyond our control" are to blame for our troubles. But this is not so. All events reflect the vibrational field in the people, places, and things that make up the events. No *accidents* happen. Preexiting low vibrational thoughts/feelings attract low vibrational experiences. And we do have dominion over our minds of thoughts/feelings. Our total system of mind-body-spirit—basically of our Self-Identity—runs our life, not a world that seems to be made up by inexplicable forces beyond our control. We have the means to solve all problems in life and be in a problem-free state all of the time.

We are *problem-solving* machines, it seems. But less obvious is that we are *problem-making* machines. In the absence of "victimhood" (or the notion that we are subject to results of external forces beyond our control), we would be 100% responsible for all things that seem to happen to us. We make up our life events with our thoughts, feelings, internal vibrations that attract them and compose them. This seems like a level of responsibility that is outrageously too broad of a scope; yet, without this complete responsibility, we would not have the wherewithal to make a complete change. There would be elements in our "change" that we could still not "change." How can we change what is beyond our control? Being 100% responsible gives us the ability to make a 100% change. Our memory jammed full of negative experiences and feelings in our life a second ago can now be altered by the reversal of our thoughts, emotions, vibrations and expectations and intentions. We have dominion over them, which determine our experiences and world. And, the first and last change we need to make is to totally forgive ourselves for the past thoughts/words/deeds and actions that have brought to us problems in the first place. We are not "sinners," but we have made some mistakes that need correction.

Let's get right down to the meaning and the implications of the word "sin." Some have said it was derived from the Greek word "hamartia" which was an archery term that meant "missing the mark." It is more at "making a mistake" than committing an infraction against Divine Laws. But "sin" has come to mean wrongdoing with a huge amount of guilt attached to it, which calls for eternal damnation. The question is then, is "sin" just a mistake easily corrected with no tinge of guilt and punishment necessary; or is it an offense to God and Higher Forces, coming with it the judgment of guilt that justifies punishment, death, and damnation? The greater implications of the latter bring about a tremendous fear of God that has arisen in people because of this false religious theology. It is no wonder that modern thinkers have thrown out the notion of God and religions altogether. What is the basis of guilt and damnation that is a result of "original sin" in our very makeup, in a world in which we are endowed with unalienable rights: Life, Liberty and the Pursuit of Happiness? The two do not *add up*.

The fundamentalist belief is that we are "original sinners" who have been benevolently relieved of our dire straits of hellish consequences through the redemption of our Savior, Jesus Christ, the "Only Son of God." We are still original sinners, but now we are "redeemed sinners." (Who by the way, "are not worthy to receive" this kind of unequivocal Grace—see in the Catholic Mass, just before receiving communion people are asked to say, "Lord, I am not worthy to receive, but only say the word and I will be healed.")

How screwed up is that!! It's a mixed message to our whole mind and psyche: we are "saved" (if we admit to being a lowly worm) but we are still "sinners" deserving of eternal damnation. The Church made up this liturgy of contradictions to control the masses of uneducated people whose taxed and tithed labors were filling the coiffeurs of their massive treasuries and worldwide organizations. While the masses were groveling in the muddy fields of agrarian survival, the orders of priests and courts of royal personages given authority by them lived comfortably in extravagance in the courts and diocese of the monied elite. Convincing people they are "sinners not worthy of receiving" kept this mythology and hierarchy of "haves" and "have nots" going well into the 20th century. It is no wonder philosophers, artists, writers, and thinkers who were somewhat divorced from this network of power began to question the status quo of "original sin" and the institutions and beliefs that kept it intact.

The perfection of what is created is always intact, no matter what imperfections are projected onto the Life-Stream, that are not even there. Two levels of the mind have to be understood to transcend the false "reality of sin." Thought in the relative mind of the ego is always dualistic. It is a realm of opposites. Love today can turn to hate tomorrow. This "love" relates to the body and its senses. Health and sickness are possible parameters of experience, accepted as equally "real." The external algorithms of diet, education, work, environment, financial success, family structures, and social interactions can affect a person to be healthy or sick. We can be conditioned to experience good health, and we can just as easily be conditioned to experience poor health. In this relative system of thought, opposites abound. Guilt from sin vs. innocence from good behavior are seen as opposites in a field of being that accepts both as plausible and *true*. This is the world of relative thought, in which we live most of the time.

Thought in the absolute Mind of God is not a world of opposites. It is a realm of effulgent Light of Truth. Truth is Pure Joy and Peace. It is not divided by conflicting thoughts and ideas. It is whole in its perfection. OM is a oneness indivisible. In this Mind, the real world is one absolved of all mistakes of dualism and opposites. In this world there are no sinners and non-sinners; there is no *heaven* to which some merit entry from a lifetime of good behavior; nor is there *hell* to which some are condemned from their dastardly deeds. There is only a collective Energy of peace and innocence which is our true inheritance, even in these dimensions of physical existence. Heaven is real, but hell is an illusion of our projection of despair upon the world. The problem is merely believing we are "separated" from our Heaven state of being which does not even have an opposite called "hell."

Forgiveness is the ending of this illusion of separation. The nature of an illusion is that it is not here. It may have appearances that seem to be here, but in the end, we see it was just a mirage of a *reality we projected.* We were just hallucinating. We were just dreaming a bad dream. And like dreaming a nightmare, when we awaken from the dream of duality and separation, we will see the Light of Truth in its wholeness. We are innocent and free of "sin" because we were created that way. God created us innocent, and we remained so. There is no black mark of "original sin" on our report cards we bring home from the school of Life.

God has condemned me not. No more do I.

My Father knows my holiness. Shall I deny His knowledge, and believe in what His knowledge makes impossible? Shall I accept as true what He proclaims as false? Or shall I take His Word for what I am, since He is my Creator, and the One Who knows the true condition of His Son?

Father, I was mistaken in myself, because I failed to realize the Source from which I came. I have not left that Source to enter in a body and to die. My holiness remains a part of me, as I am part of You. And my mistakes about myself are dreams. I let them go today. And I stand ready to receive Your Word alone for what I really am.

(ACIM; Workbook; Lesson #228)

If our Creator has not condemned us to anything, then where is the notion of "original sin" and guilt? Guilt demands punishment, so in a state where condemnation and punishment are absent, it would follow that guilt does not exist. God created us 100% innocent, in other words. This unequivocal innocence amounts to an Absolute Thought System free of opposites.

In this Mind of God, we have risen above guilt and suffering and sorrow. 100% Forgiveness is the same as taking 100% Responsibility for all results. What does not result in

Pure Joy (since there is no guilt or condemnation of any kind producing unhappiness), would have to be an illusion. And illusion, by definition, is not real. A mirage, by definition, is an illusion that appears to be real, but in the end, we find out it is not. A bad dream, which appears to grip us in its drama while we are dreaming it, vanishes into the gladdened relief of our open eyes of being awake!

Tara Singh made these two thought systems very clear to me. We battle in the unwillingness to make our decision for the absolute Thoughts of God. In the ego's world of thought, we are enmeshed in the rewards and byproducts of pleasure that remain as payoffs to our world of the duality of relative thought. We don't like the misery of experience that goes along with our life choices, yet we don't want to give up the small or large pleasures we receive from keeping our self-projected world going. So we stay in the ego's thought system even when shown the end-result is misery, suffering, and death. This unwillingness is inherent in the ego's thought system. It will always postpone a real decision and see things in perpetual shades of gray. "There is no peace except the peace of God," it says in Lesson # 200 of the Workbook, but we think somehow if we get the right combination, the right algorithm of functions just lined up correctly, we will hit the jackpot of happiness that will liberate us from our discontent. But that magical combination never occurs. Therefore the peace and happiness we seek in the world of the ego's relative thought system never come about. Perfect Peace and Happiness only exist in the field of the Absolute, and to enter into this sacred ground of our holy Mind, we have to let go of our attachment to the ego's projected world entirely.

Not so easy. This is why there are so few enlightened beings in the history of human endeavors. And the ones who do come and make this decision known, are usually crucified and fought against by the status quo of worldly reasoning. There was a great sage, Ramakrishna, (1836-1886) who made this statement:

> *The worldly-wise, when it comes to spiritual matters, always suggest a compromise.*

And the reason is the inherent unwillingness of thought to see the decision in black and white. One either forgives the world of relative thought completely and therefore steps out of it, or one stays locked in the indecision of expecting both worlds to be available to one anytime for the choosing. It is impossible to see both worlds; therefore, a decision for one—for darkness or light—must be made. And until one makes the decision for total forgiveness, some amount of blame goes on, and the world of the darkness is not escaped.

This passage further makes the case for *total forgiveness*. I take responsibility for the length of it. Being so essential, I have included this section in its entirety, and highlighted in bold the lines I feel are most important:

> ***1. The Lifting of the Veil***
>
> ***Forget not that you came this far together, you and your brother. And it was surely not the ego that led you here.*** *No obstacle to peace can be surmounted through its help. It does not open up its secrets, and bid you look on them and go beyond them. It would not have you see its weakness, and learn it has no power to keep you from the truth. The Guide Who brought you here remains with you, and when you raise your eyes you will be ready to look on terror with no fear at all. But first, lift up your eyes and look on your brother in innocence born of complete forgiveness of his illusions, and through the eyes of faith that sees them not.*
>
> ***No one can look upon the fear of God unterrified, unless he has accepted the Atonement and learned illusions are not real.*** *No one can stand before this obstacle alone, for he could not have reached this far unless his brother walked beside him. And no one would dare to look on it without complete forgiveness of his brother in his heart. Stand*

you here a while and tremble not. You will be ready. Let us join together in a holy instant, here in this place where the purpose, given in a holy instant, has led you. And let us join in faith that ***He Who brought us here together will offer you the innocence you need, and that you will accept it for my love and His.***

Nor is it possible to look on this too soon. This is the place to which everyone must come when he is ready. Once he has found his brother he is ready. Yet merely to reach the place is not enough. A journey without a purpose is still meaningless, and even when it is over it seems to make no sense. How can you know that it is over unless you realize its purpose is accomplished? Here, with the journey's end before you, you see its purpose. And it is here you choose whether to look upon it or wander on, only to return and make the choice again.

To look upon the fear of God does need some preparation. ***Only the sane can look on stark insanity and raving madness with pity and compassion, but not with fear. For only if they share in it does it seem fearful, and you do share in it until you look upon your brother with perfect faith and love and tenderness.*** *Before complete forgiveness you still stand unforgiving. You are afraid of God because you fear your brother. Those you do not forgive you fear. And no one reaches love with fear beside him.*

This brother who stands beside you still seems to be a stranger. You do not know him, and your interpretation of him is very fearful. *And you attack him still, to keep what seems to be yourself unharmed. Yet in his hands is your salvation. You see his madness, which you hate because you share it. And all the pity and forgiveness that would heal it gives way to fear.* ***Brother, you need forgiveness of your brother, for you will share in madness or in Heaven together.*** *And you will raise your eyes in faith together, or not at all.*

Beside you is one who offers you the chalice of Atonement, for the Holy Spirit is in him. Would you

hold his sins against him, or accept his gift to you? Is this giver of salvation your friend or enemy? *Choose which he is, remembering that you will receive of him according to your choice. He has in him the power to forgive your sin, as you for him. Neither can give it to himself alone. And yet your savior stands beside each one. Let him be what he is, and seek not to make of love an enemy.*

Behold your Friend, the Christ Who stands beside you. *How holy and how beautiful He is! You thought He sinned because you cast the veil of sin upon Him to hide His loveliness. Yet still He holds forgiveness out to you, to share His holiness. This "enemy," this "stranger" still offers you salvation as His Friend. The "enemies" of Christ, the worshippers of sin, know not Whom they attack.*

This is your brother, crucified by sin and waiting for release from pain. Would you not offer him forgiveness, when only he can offer it to you? *For his redemption he will give you yours, as surely as God created every living thing and loves it. And he will give it truly, for it will be both offered and received. There is no grace of Heaven that you cannot offer to your brother, and receive from your most holy Friend. Let him withhold it not, for by receiving it you offer it to him. And he will receive of you what you received of him. Redemption has been given you to give your brother, and thus receive it. Whom you forgive is free, and what you give you share. Forgive the sins your brother thinks he has committed, and all the guilt you think you see in him.*

Here is the holy place of resurrection, to which we come again; to which we will return until redemption is accomplished and received. Think who your brother is, before you would condemn him. *And offer thanks to God that he is holy, and has been given the gift of holiness for you. Join him in gladness, and remove all trace of guilt from his disturbed and tortured mind. Help him to lift the heavy burden of sin you laid upon him and he accepted as his own, and toss it lightly and with happy laughter away from him. Press it not like* *thorns against his brow, nor nail him to it, unredeemed and hopeless.*

Give faith to your brother, for faith and hope and mercy are yours to give. Into the hands that give, the gift is given. Look on your brother, and see in him the gift of God you would receive. It is almost Easter, the time of resurrection. *Let us give redemption to each other and share in it, that we may rise as one in resurrection, not separate in death. Behold the gift of freedom that I gave the Holy Spirit for you. And be you and your brother free together, as you offer to the Holy Spirit this same gift. And giving it, receive it of Him in return for what you gave. He leadeth you and me together, that we might meet here in this holy place, and make the same decision.*

Free your brother here, as I freed you. Give him the self-same gift, nor look upon him with condemnation of any kind. See him as guiltless as I look on you, and overlook the sins he thinks he sees within himself. ***Offer your brother freedom and complete release from sin, here in the garden of seeming agony and death.*** *So will we prepare together the way unto the resurrection of God's Son, and let him rise again to glad remembrance of his Father, Who knows no sin, no death, but only life eternal.*

Together we will disappear into the Presence beyond the veil, not to be lost but found; not to be seen but known. And knowing, nothing in the plan God has established for salvation will be left undone. *This is the journey's purpose, without which is the journey meaningless. Here is the peace of God, given to you eternally by Him. Here is the rest and quiet that you seek, the reason for the journey from its beginning.* ***Heaven is the gift you owe your brother, the debt of gratitude you offer to the Son of God in thanks for what he is, and what his Father created him to be.***

Think carefully how you would look upon the giver of this gift, for as you look on him so will the gift itself appear to be. As he is seen as either the giver of guilt or salvation, so will his offering be seen and so received. ***The crucified give pain because they are in pain. But the redeemed give joy because they have been healed of pain. Everyone gives as he receives, but he must choose what it will* be *that he receives.*** *And he will recognize his choice by what he gives, and what is given him. Nor is it given anything in hell or Heaven to interfere with his decision.*

You came this far because the journey was your choice. And no one undertakes to do what he believes is meaningless. What you had faith in still is faithful, and watches over you in faith so gentle yet so strong that it would lift you far beyond the veil, and place the Son of God safely within the sure protection of his Father. Here is the only purpose that gives this world, and the long journey through this world, whatever meaning lies in them. Beyond this, they are meaningless. ***You and your brother stand together, still without conviction they have a purpose. Yet it is given you to see this purpose in your holy Friend, and recognize it as your own.***

(ACIM: Text; Chapter 19; Section IV D; ¶8-21)

Recently, I had a situation in which a student became very angry with Sondra and me on the India Quest. This student and we were working together in our worldwide Liberation Breathing mission. We wanted to re-establish our sovereignty of the administration end of the mission, over which he was gradually taking more control. There were some other corrections we needed to make with him, which we did. Then he went ballistic on us. Threats and insults ensued from his language and behavior. What to do? The anger levels were greater than we had ever witnessed. How were we to apply complete forgiveness to this situation? How were we to not go into fear? We let the situation simmer for a while.

In the crisis of the moment, after three days of unrelenting anger, we asked him to leave the India Quest. But this was only a "temporary fix." In the light of the above passages, and others in *ACIM*, complete forgiveness depends on my applying innocence to this person with whom we had this angry exchange. We did not attack back, but we did remove him immediately from others in our group, and ourselves, with whom his sustained anger was beginning to adversely affect. This decision was made with the input of another wise person in the ashram at Herakhan, namely the head of the entire ashram.

You may have some similar encounter with a person in your life in which a very dramatic contrast of anger and separation seems to loom large. This could be current, or in your memory of failed relationships. For me, this person, especially if I claim to be a student of *A Course in Miracles*, was not sent to me by accident. In fact, the Holy Spirit sent him there in my space to test my levels of forgiveness. Is my forgiveness complete or not? And if I desire to make it complete, how will I see this person in the light beyond the crisis?

Anger, control, and domination are the ego's version of power. But fear of anger, control and domination are not far behind in this dynamic. Fear of what another can do to you with motives that are not in your best interests can be just as damaging as the motives themselves. Now that the dust has settled upon the critical action of a practical separation to stop the escalation of anger, what is the right response of the Holy Spirit to arrive at complete and total forgiveness?

In Lesson #78, Jesus asks us to bring to mind such a person with whom we have had extreme difficulty. Someone whom we may see as harmful to us and our world. And he asks us to apply this prayer:

Let me behold my savior in this one
You have appointed as the one for me
to ask to lead me to the holy light
in which he stands, that I may join with him.

Not only is Jesus asking us to love our enemy as ourselves, here He is taking us one step farther in our forgiveness process to see our enemy as our *savior*. Well, *A Course in Miracles* is not for the faint of heart. Can I do it? Can you do it? Will we do it? The challenge is here. Do we want to rise to the level of the Christ in us or not? Do I want to? The test is upon me.

Our words are for the most part timid gestures and meaningless thoughts. What is the real Action of Life? I am in the midst of it here and now. What would a real Action of Life reveal to me? It begins with a heartfelt invocation:

> *Remembering this, let us devote the remainder of the extended practice periods to asking God to reveal His plan to us. Ask Him very specifically:*
>
> ***What would you have me do?***
> ***Where would you have me go?***
> ***What would you have me say, and to whom?***
>
> *Give Him full charge of the rest of the practice period, and let Him tell you what needs to be done by you in His plan for your salvation. He will answer in proportion to your willingness to hear His Voice. Refuse not to hear. The very fact that you are doing the exercises proves that you have some willingness to listen. This is enough to establish your claim to God's answer.*
>
> *(ACIM; Workbook; Lesson #71)*

Okay. Am I going to listen to a plan that is not my own, God's plan for salvation, or am I going to insist I know best? Here we are brought to the juncture of our humility: that God knows what I am to do, but I do not. Can we approach an invocation with this amount of surrender, and willingness to hear "an Answer" that is not born of our thought system?

Okay. I *am willing* to open myself up and hear the Answer to these questions concerning the student we had to ask to leave the India Quest. Here is the Answer.

Dear ________,

I need to communicate some things.

- *I am sorry.*
- *Please forgive me.*
- *I Love you.*
- *Thank You.*

There is nothing to do now between us. And there is nowhere to go in the physical dimensions together. Our work with you is complete on these levels. The proper completion of a cycle is done.

Alas, there is still something to say, as God would have us be brothers, and enter that final Gate to Heaven together or not at all. And in the dimension of time, this entrance is NOW, the only real-time there is.

"All things are lessons God would have me learn." (Lesson #193 in ACIM) And therefore our exchanges in Herakhan were God sent. I do not doubt this. They had the hand of Sri Babaji upon them, as well as the hand of Greater Wisdom that neither of us fully possessed at the time.

Meeting the adversities of thoughts and experiences with anger is never justified. Yet, meeting anger with even a tinge of fear is neither justified. And I must say that your expressions of anger scared the shit out of me, to be frank. But so be it. Thank you for scaring the shit out of me. I doubt that any amount of anger will ever do that to me again, having really and deeply processed this in myself.

In the area of Sondra's and my work together, we are led. This is not a speculation, but a fact, forged in the fires of spiritual dedication to our processes for many years. For Sondra this dedication began in 1963 when she joined the Peace Corps and served the people in the jungles of Peru; in 1968 as an Air Force nurse tending to the grief in the families of Vietnam pilots killed in action; and later in 1974 when she was the third person in line for the "great experiment" of Rebirthing to be awakened in the breath. For me, this journey began in 1982, when I became aware of my spiritual quest after finishing graduate school in art; in 1987 when I journeyed to India to Babaji's feet for the first time; and in 1989 when I met my teacher of A Course in Miracles, Tara Singh, to whom I was loyal as my teacher for 17 years, until his passing in 2006. Sondra and I bowed our heads on this journey to the Self back then, and we never lifted them.

As teachers, we are also students. In fact, the best teachers are merely the best students. And we are honored to be the students. All of our actions as teachers are to be the true students who can surrender to a Wisdom Greater than our own.

In the events that transpired on the India Quest between you and us, we are eternally grateful. We had to draw a line in the area of boundaries: what we would accept as a behavior of any participant going through their process on the Quest—and what we would not accept. Thank you for teaching us this lesson. Thank you for showing us our strength to draw this line and establish this boundary.

In the area of money, thank you also for bringing us to clarity in that department. We are grateful that the Masters always provide for us financially for our work and life—we always have a favorable balance of trade, and all of our bills are paid without effort, and we hold no debt whatsoever in our life. We are clear and in the flow, whether our results are astronomical or modest. The human being comes first in what we do. We serve the people. And it is our greatest joy to do so. And we do this with an austere abundance that flows from Divine Providence.

Sondra and I live in the vibration of Simplicity, a major pillar in Sri Babaji's teachings. This is consistent as well with the teachings of my Master, Tara Singh, who had this Chinese Proverb in his Foundation:

We never buy more than we need.
We never need more than we use.
We never use more than it takes to get by
Till we learn to need less.

And at the same time, we never deny ourselves the excellence of anything we desire for the fulfillment of our Joy.

As far as the organization and management of our work around the world, again, we defer to those Higher Powers of the Masters Who guide us. We need no other "managers" or purveyors of good practices. We apologize for giving you the impression that we did. Karma Yoga, as you know, is to give all acts of work to the Divine Will without the ulterior motives of any specific return or results. In effect, the true Karma Yogi is not even attached to results. He is employing pure means, which are motiveless. As far as these pure means, we are grateful for lessons of organization and management that you suggested that increase our effectiveness to spread our message around the world. Thank you.

In the department of telling me I'm fat, Churchill was fat and an alcoholic too, and defeated Hitler who was svelte and a vegetarian. And Babaji was fat as well in the latter years of his mission. Weight goes up and weight goes down. So I am innocent of whatever the shape of my body. The highest Yoga, Raja Yoga, begins and ends in the mind, and Vivekananda, the most astute voice on this Yoga, was robust in body. Ammachi has extra pounds, and she loves people by the millions. So I feel in good company here, to be un-swayed by this modern era's obsession with weight and physical looks. But thanks anyway for trying to insult me in that area, as it helped me to get clear I am AOK just as I am, in whatever body I manifest at this moment.

We wish you well in your future with your lady, _________. She is a fine person to stick by you in a crisis such as the one we experienced in Herakhan with you. When all is said and done, you know where we stand in the Spiritual Intimacy of monogamy, in the vibration of a conflict-free relationship. This is what we embrace and this is what Sondra and I write openly about. And if that one lesson enters your field of awareness, we are glad. We certainly wish you and ________ to have this Spiritual Intimacy that is true and lasting. It is the source of our Pure Joy, and we wish that for you two as well. It is our "heaven on earth." And once in heaven, why would we ever want to amend it or add to it or leave it in any way? We would not. It is complete and whole in every way. Om Shanti!

To close, Thank You and God bless you for all the many lessons you delivered that God would have us learn. We hold you in high regard as a student and as a teacher of the one lesson of complete forgiveness to us in our process of ascension. If "Love is the way we walk in gratitude" (Lesson #195 in ACIM), you are an integral part of our walk, towards a "Peace that surpasses understanding."

Godspeed, ________.

Markus Ray & Sondra Ray

Washington DC.
April 28, 2019

This is the letter I sent to my brother whose anger scared the shit out of me. The actions were correct to ask him to leave the ashram for the benefit of the other India Quest participants, but I needed to take responsibility for any fear I had in the face of his anger. Total forgiveness of the "fear of God" that we project onto our angry brothers is necessary to be the Christ. Only loving thoughts are true, and everything else is a call for help, even when we find ourselves the object of another's attacks.

To look at extreme anger directed towards us without retaliating or defending ourselves is the epitome of Lesson #153, "In my defenselessness my safety lies." And, as *The Lifting of the Veil* cited above points out:

Only the sane can look on stark insanity and raving madness with pity and compassion, but not with fear.

It was a great test for me. I flunked a little in the moment, but I was shown the error and I am grateful for the Love of Correction that Tara Singh gave to me.

Total Forgiveness is a process in our life that will attract many lessons God would have us learn. We do not shed all fear over-night, just because we know *it is not justified*. The memories of *fight or flight* are in our brain constitution from time immemorial. So we will be tested with situations to rewire the very genetic structure of our internal guidance system. This is beyond the brain memory of what is merely recorded. It requires a mutation—in which miracles are needed—to lift us out of the conditioned responses.

How we respond in the face of someone going ballistic toward us is a great test. Here are some helpful directions I used. A stop-action is necessary first. Take yourself out of harm's way. Or maybe a boundary has to be drawn, a strong boundary. Or what therapists call "tough love" needs to be exercised. Bringing something to a head can precipitate anger in others. So brace yourself when you are going to speak the truth to someone who does not want to hear it. This person may react with the anger of unpredictable intensity.

Then:

Face it down.
Don't look away.
Don't engage with a "comeback."
See your Savior in this one.
Let the person have his say.
Stay in your calm.
No fear.
Take an action, if necessary.
(Remove yourself or the other)

And later:

Ask yourself the errors (thoughts) in yourself that attracted this to you.
Make a list of a half dozen points.
Write affirmations to turn these errors around.

And when you are feeling really strong:

Write the person a letter of Ho'oponopono and Gratitude. Ho'oponopono premises your communication:

Dear ________.

I need to communicate some things.

I am sorry.
Please forgive me.
I Love you.
Thank You.

Then include your Letter of Gratitude. (Example above) This final response should diffuse the situation (that has had some days or weeks to simmer down). Taking these steps will bring you closer to total forgiveness, and closer to your True Self as the Christ. We must always remember when feeling attacked:

Forgiveness should be practiced through the day, for there will still be many times when you forget its meaning and attack yourself. When this occurs, allow your mind to see through this illusion as you tell yourself:

Let me perceive forgiveness as it is. Would I accuse myself of doing this? I will not lay this chain upon myself.

In everything you do remember this:

No one is crucified alone, and yet no one can enter Heaven by himself.

(ACIM; Workbook; Lesson #134)

This will complete the cycle. You may or may not have physical dealings with this person again, but that does not matter. Because you have got the lesson and done the deep forgiveness work, your purpose for being together could be done. Total forgiveness does not mean to re-engage in another cycle that may result in the same explosions. You have to be wise in this area too.

Total forgiveness is mostly for us. Any grievances still held affect our receptivity of unconditional Love. Our grievances block this awareness in us. Our grievances are an attack on unconditional Love. So which do we want—hang on to our grievances and suffer, or let them go and awaken into the Peace of God in us? The choice is always ours.

PART 2

The Work Required

6.
Who Do We Hate?

The notion of progress is an illusion. Tara Singh shares in the talks he gave called "What Is The Christ?" comments about his own teacher's words on this subject of progress. I am paraphrasing them here:

> *Krishnamurti pointed out that in the Roman times it cost a few hundred dollars to train a soldier; in modern times it costs thousands of dollars to train a soldier. A few millennia ago someone said the bow and arrow could do a much better job to kill a man than a club. Now we have the nuclear bomb that can annihilate millions at once. And we call that progress. He went on to say that in the past 50,000 years mankind has hardly progressed at all. Man may have evolved in the opposite direction. Apparently, he may have devolved. This is the sad state of affairs. And technology cannot solve this issue. It is one of an internal nature and has to be addressed at the source of the problem—in the very psychological makeup of the human being.*

When one asks *why*, and then looks at the conditions in the human being that precipitated this insane illusion of progress, conditions that accept mass killing as a very possible result of our actions, then the whole system of progress becomes tainted with the sheer facts of possible human annihilation. Tara Singh went on to say that "Affluence without Wisdom is Self-Destructive." We can certainly observe that.

The notion that there is an enemy, one in competition with our best interests, goes back to territorial rights and sexual rights of early social groups. The rights to the herd, the water hole, the good grazing land, the premier location for the tribe, and the mating rites to the best females organized people around the smartest, fittest and strongest members of the tribe. This is the animal kingdom's evolution of natural selection that ensured the "survival of the fittest." Within this dynamic of control and domination, the most violent and assertive people ruled over the lesser, more peaceful and meeker folks. At the purely physical level, humans acted upon their animal tendencies—and anger, domination, and control became the definition of individual and social "power" as well.

Who do we hate? Growing up in the 1960s we were taught in the USA that Russians were not only bad people, but they were also going to blow us up with nuclear bombs someday. We did various drills in our school in which we lined up in the basement so we would somehow be protected from fallout and other horrendous conditions of nuclear war. It was all preposterous of course, but it gave us a sense of "something to fear," and that we had to be prepared for the worse.

Wars are promoted via the notion that whole groups of people, whole countries are evil enemies against the best interests of our people, our country, our way of life. Nationalism is just an expanded manifestation of tribalism. *Our people* and tribe are better deserving of life's graces than *your people* and tribe. Our religion and beliefs are more true and holy than your religion and beliefs. It is an observable phenomenon that national, political, and religious interests divide mankind into separate factions and groups. And sometimes the friction between these groups is escalated to the level of war. Even in the "cold war" we were not only frightened in the USA of what the Soviets could do to us but with "God on our side," we certainly thought we were on the side of the *right*. Those "godless communists" were evil people whom we had every right to hate. And with God on our side, we had every right to build up a massive military-industrial complex, and assure that we could win any war against our enemies—those phantom people halfway around the world who were "out to get us," and of course, deserving of our hatred. Well, few saw the ridiculousness of this popular notion. People tend to want an enemy. We seem to "love to hate" someone.

> *You never hate your brother for his sins, but only for your own. Whatever form his sins appear to take, it but obscures the fact that you believe it to be yours, and therefore meriting a "just" attack.*
>
> *Why should his sins be sins, if you did not believe they could not be forgiven in you? Why are they real in him, if you did not believe that they are your reality? And why do you attack them everywhere except you hate yourself? Are* you *a sin? You answer "yes" whenever you attack, for by attack do you assert that you are guilty, and must give as you deserve. And what can you deserve but what you are? If you did not believe that you deserved attack, it never would occur to you to give attack to anyone at all. Why should you? What would be the gain to you? What could the outcome be that you would want? And how could murder bring you benefit?*
>
> *(ACIM; Text; Chapter 3; Section III; ¶ 1-2)*

This is a completely different view on the object of our hate. It is from a section in the *Course* called *The Self-Accused*. Most of us know the saying, "When you point the finger at someone else three fingers are pointing back at you." This passage takes it a step farther: "You never hate your brother for his sins, but only for your own." One could not hate, in other words, unless there was tremendous self-hate already in us. To attack another with hate is to attack ourselves. This is a law.

Today I learn the law of love; that what I give my brother, is my gift to me.
(ACIM; Workbook; Lesson #344)

How long will it take humanity to wake up? As we give out we receive. If we give out aggression, domination, and control, we will be ruled by the fear that makes us want to dominate and control in the first place. As we attack another, we will be attacking ourselves. There is no "other."

We cannot wait for society to change. The shift in consciousness has to begin in you and me. Society is an abstract conglomeration of individuals expressing the collective tendencies of each of its members. Therefore, the change must begin in each one of us to see things differently. And this change, to be a real change, must happen NOW, in the present. If we put it off until later, real change will never happen. We could say it is a good idea to give up hate, but if we do not look at the hate within ourselves and transmute it now, it will continue, unexamined. We would keep adding to the hate we see "out there" in "society."

What steps do we need to take in this action to give up hate? Together we can look at them. It is a *collaborative venture.*

7. The Law of Love

What is the law? We can expect that a law is a true principle, and because of that truth, worthy of being followed. In the worldly sense the dictionary defines it like this:

> *The system of rules which a particular country or community recognizes as regulating the actions of its members and which it may enforce by the imposition of penalties: they were taken to court for breaking the law.*

A "system of rules" is made up by a governing body of men and women for the good of the whole society, presumably. But we have seen man-made rules may not always serve the greater good of the whole—such as the *Jim Crow Laws* before the 1960s in America, that subjugated the black community in the South to inequalities and social suppression. So, a *system of rules* is not necessarily just, for the benefit of all. It may favor the few, or those holding the power to make the rules, to the detriment of a large body of people. Laws of the governing body of the

Revolutionary governments can too often abuse their power and send a lot of innocent people to their deaths. Over and over history shows and repeats this.

The other implication is that those who "break the laws" will be dealt with by punishment or *penalties*. Laws are to be followed with the fear that not following them will bring about dire and painful consequences. The problem with this definition of "law" is that fear is instigated as a governing factor in the following of the law, and punishment and guilt are meted out to the non-conformists.

Is there a *Higher Law*, one that is not subject to the inequities of the man-made rules that are potentially self-serving of the few in power? Is there a *Higher Law* that does not use the fear of punishment and the guilt of "breaking the rules" as the impetus for obedience?

Is there such a thing as a Divine Law? The Creation that holds the stars and the Cosmos intact has unseen forces that keep the planets from colliding. There is a *Force of Life* that keeps our heartbeat going and allows our breath to take in the vital substance even when we are not thinking about these necessary functions. What is this Life Force, and how can we make contact with the "laws" that govern it? This is a *system of rules* not subject to the regulations of governments and man-made groups of legislation.

These are not merely Natural Laws either. One could observe the law of natural selection in which the survival of the fittest rules the reproductive behaviors of the herd, the flock, the group of any particular species. There is the law of gravity in which larger bodies have an attractive pull upon smaller bodies. This affects water here on earth, which makes it flow downhill. These are Natural Laws that are observable.

But are there even Higher Laws? These are laws that are not subject to even Natural Laws which appear to be immutable. The Wisdom of *A Course in Miracles* puts forth this declaration of independence:

I am under no laws but God's.
(ACIM; Workbook; Lesson #76)

What is the "Law of God?" Jesus says this is the only law that we are required to obey. It is not necessarily exclusive of laws we discussed above, but it is a *Higher Law*, a *Law* which transcends all others.

> *Think of the freedom in the recognition that you are not bound by all the strange and twisted laws you have set up to save you. You really think that you would starve unless you have stacks of green paper strips and piles of metal discs. You really think a small round pellet or some fluid pushed into your veins through a sharpened needle will ward off disease and death. You really think you are alone unless another body is with you.*
>
> *It is insanity that thinks these things. You call them laws, and put them under different names in a long catalog of rituals that have no use and serve no purpose. You think you must obey the "laws" of medicine, of economics and of health. Protect the body, and you will be saved. (ACIM; Workbook; Lesson #76)*

The laws under which we think we live are mostly physical laws of medicine, economics, and social interaction.

> *These are not laws, but madness. The body is endangered by the mind that hurts itself. The body suffers just in order that the mind will fail to see it is the victim of itself. The body's suffering is a mask the mind holds up to hide what really suffers. It would not understand it is its own enemy; that it attacks itself and wants to die. It is from this your "laws" would save the body. It is for this you think you are a body. (ACIM; Workbook; Lesson #76)*

Most rules by which we live pertain to the body, and to the mind which thinks it is in service of the body, under its "laws." These are pretty strong words in Jesus's indictment of our misplaced allegiances. The mind does not see it is hurting itself by believing in suffering, and being a victim of suffering that it made up itself. It did not see itself as the culprit, and "laws" designed to protect us from suffering do not really work.

> *There are no laws except the laws of God. This needs repeating, over and over, until you realize it applies to everything that you have made in opposition to God's Will. Your magic has no meaning. What it is meant to save does not exist. Only what it is meant to hide will save you.*
>
> *The laws of God can never be replaced. We will devote today to rejoicing that this is so. It is no longer a truth we would hide. We realize instead it is a truth that keeps us free forever. Magic imprisons, but the laws of God make free. The light has come because there are no laws but His. (ACIM; WB; Lesson #76)*

Joy, Freedom, and Light are the inevitable results of God's laws. But we have to get clear about the true function of our mind. Are we using the mind in service of the Spirit or of the Body, mainly?

Self-Identity is an awareness of who we are. Who we are is our Source, and our mind in service to this Source is properly aligned. Our body in service to this Source is also properly aligned. And when the mind/body is connected to its Spiritual Source, there is only one Law under which it abides. This is the *Law of Love*, the *Law of God*, or the "law of giving."

God's laws forever give and never take.
(ACIM; Workbook; Lesson #76)

This is very profound. Giving is at the basis of God's laws. Love is a giving in action. It is an extension of the Light and Joy and Peace that we begin to associate with the Life Force, and with our life. We are under no laws but God's because we were created in the same vibration of this *Law of Love*.

Now that we see the *Law of Love* is an act of giving, we must clear up the misperception we have about giving as well. In the "laws of the world," we give to get. Or, what we give away we no longer have, therefore giving is seen as either with a motive to "get something in return," or it is an act whereby what we give away we no longer have anymore.

A Course in Miracles presents a different view of giving. We give what we already have, and by giving it we realize we have it. So, in the giving, there is an increase in what we have. I have love in myself, let's say. By giving it to you, I realize that I already have it, and in the giving, I receive more love into my awareness. So this is the basic "Law of Love:"

To give and to receive are one in truth.
(ACIM; Workbook; Lesson #108)

How does this make you feel? It gets us in the vibration of abundance, of self-esteem, of having all that we need to realize and extend the good life. Giving is the *law of God*, and by this law do all things live. It is a cycle of receiving and giving that is demonstrated even in the Natural World—the tree receives the rain, the soil, the light, and the CO2, and in turn, it gives the home for animals, the wood for our needs, and oxygen for life. In this way of giving, life is a constant exchange of joy.

Today I learn the law of Love, that what I give my brother is my gift to me.
(ACIM; Workbook; Lesson #344)

We are uplifted by this law I mentioned in Chapter 6; at the same time, we are asked to be responsible for what we give because it will come back to us in due proportion. Giving is the *Law of Love*. Can we be aware of this basic principle and joyously apply it? The returns will be remarkable!

8. The Work of Forgiveness

We have obviously not always given to ourselves and others the joy and the happiness of life. This is obvious. We have too often given judgment, anger, disappointment, and a cache of negative thoughts and emotions for which we often felt fully justified. But these did not make us feel good. In the aftermath of these negative emotional exchanges, we felt depressed, lonely, regretful, sorry, and low. Amidst these emotional exchanges, we have wallowed in the quagmire of problems, which felt beyond our control to solve.

The Second Coming is clarity about the solution. It is an escape out of the victim consciousness that thinks, "This bad thing is happening to me from outside forces beyond my control." The Second Coming gives us the clarity of full responsibility which says, "There is part of my subconscious mind, or vibration in myself, which attracted this negative problem; therefore I can change my mind to dissolve it."

An Enlightened Being usually has a particular lesson to impart to humanity. We can observe this in their mission as the highlights of what they said and what they did. Jesus came to impart the real truth about Forgiveness. Two thousand years ago He was being crucified on the cross by the Romans (and by the belligerent rulers of his Jewish community), and He said to God while hanging in pain on the cross, "Forgive them for they know not what they are doing." The fact that He knew they were operating with an insane and cruel mind of relative thought, separated from the Rational and Loving mind of Absolute Thought, He did not hold that against them. He knew this was the status quo of limited consciousness most people possess. He came to correct this mistake—that human beings are stuck in this duality of good versus evil, and attack what does not satisfy them, deeming it evil. Jesus operated in the Absolute Thought system of God. The relative thought has no meaning at this level—therefore how could He hold anything against His attackers. They couldn't do anything but attack Him, Who represented the higher *Law of Love.* Therefore, He represented forgiveness in the Absolute sense. He did not even see their errors as real, even though His physical suffering was a result of their mistakes.

A *Course in Miracles* picks up this theme of forgiveness, and the result is the Atonement when forgiveness is complete. It also establishes the Christ as the one in charge of this process:

> *I am in charge of the process of Atonement, which I undertook to begin. When you offer a miracle to any of my brothers, you do it to* yourself *and me.*
>
> *(ACIM; Text; Chapter 1; Section III; ¶ 1)*

Christ is available to us directly. We will go through our own processes of forgiveness, the sum total of which adds up to the Atonement. Each time we let go of a "grievance," or see our part in making up a "problem," we are moving in the direction of the state of total forgiveness. In this state of total forgiveness, we are absolved of all errors and have a vision of our innocence, our real Self. In this way, we are joined with Christ in the correction of all thoughts of non-love. The beauty of this is we are not alone. Jesus is there every step of the way holding our hand, guiding us, giving us the help we need to let go. We have the power to work miracles through Him, but we have to be listening to Him. We have a natural power to work miracles, but we need to gain confidence in our ability to turn things around. When we allow the Holy Spirit to do this for us, only our "little willingness" is needed as a catalyst for change. Christ gives us forgiveness as our purpose as well.

The Christ is "in charge of the process of Atonement." Atonement is the correction of all errors in our minds. It is also a unification of Spirit/Mind/Body. It is also the unification of the "Sonship," which is the Whole Divine Body of the human race.

What is the implication of Atonement in terms of forgiveness? The "canceling out of all errors" is an act of forgiveness. It cancels any "wrongdoing" with the correction of right-mindedness. Therefore, it employs pardon instead of condemnation and punishment as its principle means. Pardon is always justified in the realm of forgiveness. Attack and punishment are never justified. How can this be, which is so different than the notion of "justice" in the world?

The real forgiveness is in seeing that there are two thought systems—one of the relative thought system of the ego, one based on opposites—and one of the Absolute Thought System of the Holy Spirit, the one of total unification in Truth. In the first system, there is constant attack and conflict; in the second there is total peace, free of any conflict. Forgiveness then is merely the decision to give up the first thought system for the second one.

The reason it feels like "work" is that we are very unwilling to let go of being "right," or feeling we were "unfairly treated," or being "the victim," or thinking we are the righteous ones in an unrighteous situation. Tara Singh, my teacher of *A Course in Miracles*, said, "Unwillingness rules." And until we face this in ourselves, and undo it, then the pain and suffering of our relative thought system will prevail.

How does one overcome unwillingness? Well, first we have to see we have it. Then we have to see it keeps us in suffering. Then we have to decide to give up our suffering. It is all about making a decision. And a decision is something sacred, one we make with our Creator. It is different from a mere "choice." It is not a casual thing. Nor is it a fanatic thing that requires some kind of delirious dedication. It is a gentle knowing that thought can only go so far in the undoing of thought—the relative system we live by. Knowing this we give attention to this moment of suspended animation of thought. Call it awareness. It is a "knowing" of the fact we do not "know." Unwillingness thinks it "knows." It has all kinds of activities that will improve us, and make us "better." But all these activities are children of unwillingness.

The work of Forgiveness is to bring our minds to emptiness—to stillness—to silence. This is the easiest thing because it is not a "doing," but it is the hardest thing to the ego that is preoccupied all of the time with its "doings" and "knowings." Ihaleakala, one of my teachers of Ho'oponopono—a Hawaiian Forgiveness Process of inner cleansing—once said at the root of the "forgiveness problem" is the fact that "people do not know that they don't know." True forgiveness, then, begins with a relinquishment of our ego's "knowing." Krishnamurti espoused the same—that true wisdom begins with "Freedom from the known." My master Tara Singh said, "What is it you know? You know how to be selfish, insecure, fearful, and problem-ridden." So more "knowing" is not going to liberate us from our internal conundrums. What we have accumulated as knowledge is the main source of all the problems we face. Undoing them must come from a different place, free from the "known."

This undoing process within us is the action and work of Forgiveness. It is an inner correction introduced by our *little willingness* to make contact with the truth of the unknown. We somehow know something is amiss in our shortfall from bliss. We have more than an inkling that the purpose of our life could be much more rounded out by the focus of Divine attention we have yet to master. This is the working aspect of letting go. Tara Singh referred to this by saying we must "resign" ourselves to the fact we do not know what true Love is. And in that admission are all things corrected, and the advent of our true Self can enter into our awareness. This is the work of Forgiveness. It is essential in our ascent to be Who we are as God created us—the Christ.

9.
The Gifts of God

Peace, Happiness, A Quiet Mind, A Certainty of Purpose, A Sense of Worth and Beauty that Transcends the World, Care, Safety, The Warmth of Sure Protection Always, A Quietness that Cannot Be Disturbed, A Gentleness that Never Can Be Hurt, A Deep Abiding Comfort, and A Rest So Perfect It Can Never Be Upset—these are the *Gifts of God*. They are made clear by the Christ in Lesson #122 of *A Course in Miracles*: "Forgiveness offers everything I want," in the first paragraph.

Who has received these *Gifts* in the Absolute sense in which they are meant to be received? Probably so few even would ponder them as gifts, sloughing them off as something too general to be of value. We like to talk about peace or happiness but who is truly at peace? Who is truly happy all of the time? This is the nature of the *Gifts of God*—they are Absolute—therefore they are constant, and never revert to the opposite. The peace of God does not have a "war of God" as its counterpart. Nor does the Happiness God bestows upon us have a "sorrow of God" into which we may fall. The Absolute means that it has no opposite. It stands outside the chops and changes of time. It is what it is—past, present, and future. It is unaffected by time at all. It is Timeless in the greatest sense of the word—unaffected by time and change.

When I first read *A Course in Miracles* and did the Lessons in the Workbook for the first time, I did not even remember these "Gifts of God" from Lesson #122. My attention was not deep enough to receive the *Gifts*. Other lessons refer to the *Gifts of God*. In fact, Lesson # 166 says, "I am entrusted with the Gifts of God." When I read that Lesson years ago I began to question myself. "Just what are these *gifts* I am entrusted with?" The yearning to know got stronger and stronger in me. Somehow, when the question is real, the answer is given. I blundered one day into Lesson #122 and saw them staring me in the face. There were twelve of them shining like jewels:

1. Peace
2. Happiness
3. A Quiet Mind
4. A Certainty of Purpose
5. A Sense of Worth and Beauty that Transcends the World
6. Care
7. Safety
8. The Warmth of Sure Protection Always
9. A Quietness that Cannot Be Disturbed
10. A Gentleness That Never Can Be Hurt
11. A Deep Abiding Comfort
12. A Rest So Perfect It Can Never Be Upset

What we all must see in reading this list is that our realization of these states of being is mostly partial—meaning it is not constant, full, and all of the time. We may be at peace sometimes, but a great part of the time we are in some sort of turmoil or conflict—either with others or even with ourselves. We may experience happiness sometimes, but in general, we are most of the time chasing some external conditions that will give us some sense of greater happiness. Therefore, even our happiness stays at the "level of pursuit." Honestly, we are chasing something we do not feel we fully have, therefore the pursuit itself is an indication that the elusive fish of happiness has escaped us, for the most part, as a constant realization.

As for a quiet mind, who has that? Our minds are so preoccupied with so many motives and concerns. Who has emptied their minds adequately enough for it to be silenced? And with the silence of thought, who can say their mind is quiet? Probably no one.

"A certainty of purpose" is something more than a career or a family. Everyone has those already. But do we ask ourselves what our greater purpose in life is, and are we certain we are living out that purpose? Service of some kind is a purpose. Service to the whole of humanity most likely would employ the talents and interests we already have. There is no "sacrifice" in a purposeful life. When we are mostly with our true purpose we are also peaceful and happy. Our minds are "quiet" in that there is no conflict in a "certainty of purpose." Certainty by its very nature does not have opposing views or doubts. That is why it is certain. Therefore, it is one pointed, focused on a direction that is conducive to the fulfillment of our highest life purpose.

"A sense of worth and beauty that transcends the world" is the ultimate statement of self-esteem. A person with this sense has risen above all self-judgments, and most likely judgments of others as well. He or she exists in the vibration of beauty, value, reality that is unaffected by external circumstances. This kind of person has an appreciation for life, and they are happy, productive people. What they do, they do in certainty it is for their good, and the good of all. And they know they are contributing to a better world, one that transcends all the problems and cynicism that plague most critiques of the human condition.

Care. Who cares? What cares? Do you care? Do you feel cared for in your world? Does God care? Do you feel that God cares for you specifically, or are you just floating in a kind of cosmic soup of existence left by yourself to experience whatever life sends down the pike for you to field and cope with on your own? This issue of care is very important. Usually, we feel cared for most when our life is clipping along pretty good, and our actions are producing the benefits and accomplishments we deem our principle purpose here. But what about when things go awry? Then who cares? This is when we need most of this sense of care. Often it is remedial on our part, as we find ourselves nurturing ourselves on our own without the help or care of others, let alone from a benevolent life force we call God. Well, so much for "care." If we want it we have to get it from the orderly lifestyle we have already set up for ourselves.

Safety. Now there's a big one. Who feels safe? Most of the time we are riding shotgun over the stagecoach of our life while expecting bandits and highwaymen just around the corner to confiscate our cargo of gold we spent so long and hard accumulating. No way on the safety thing. We are mostly safe to the degree we have planned our trip out well on predictable coach roads, and our guns are so big and drawn out in plain sight that no one dares to mess with our self-made tranquility out of fear that they will get totally blasted at the first sign of overstepping into our space of self-possessions. We fought hard to get this place of *safety*, and no threats will penetrate our defenses. We are safe to the degree we carry a big stick.

"The warmth of sure protection always" is quite a poetic way of saying we are feeling good that nothing can intrude upon our world we made up. Being that as it is, we don't believe we are that invulnerable to attack, or shifts of fate, or small or large cataclysms of circumstances beyond our control.

More often we feel the cold hard heart of indifference in which things can go badly off, more than we feel the "warmth of sure protection." So much for that one.

"A quietness that cannot be disturbed" would have to be mighty quiet. And in the cacophonous din of daily life, this is not so easy to say we can do it—put ourselves in that deep quiet without being catatonic. Ignorance is bliss, but in this case, we are talking about being fully aware of our peace within, and also abreast of the "war without," which does not disturb us in the least of ways. We are talking about something almost supernatural here. Who can remain totally calm in the face of a total blast of disaster? This would be a test for anyone who prides themselves on the virtues of meditation and mindfulness. Who is absolutely quiet? Not too many; and how do we get there ourselves to receive this *Gift of God*?

"A gentleness that never can be hurt" is quite a statement. We normally associate safety with "having a big stick," as I said. So defenses and safety are all wired together in the ego's world of self-government. "Kindness is confused with weakness," as the saying goes. So we pride ourselves in not being too kind and gentle, lest we be perceived as weak and our vulnerability leaves us wide open for attack. In the Holy Spirit's view of things the opposite is the case: Defenses attract attack; they do not deter them. Therefore to be defenseless is safety—"In my defenselessness my safety lies." Lesson #153 in *ACIM* Workbook. What could be farther from the worldly view—that defenses make a person, tribe, a country strong. We, therefore, have tremendous "defense budgets" that have little to do with gentleness.

"A deep abiding comfort" is rarely associated with being defenseless. *Deep* means at the very core of our bones, and *abiding* means that it is a pervading quality that sticks around and never leaves us. *Comfort* is a sense of physical well-being and lack of strain of any kind. A *deep abiding comfort* is like saying you feel good all the time. Never are you in a state of duress or pain, and you feel comfortable in your skin no matter what the situation may bring. Who has this comfort?

"A rest so perfect it can never be upset." What is this perfect rest? Have we ever had it? It is like "perfect happiness." We are not talking about a state of being that can be here today and gone tomorrow. Never means never. So any upset that may come along is deterred by perfect rest. Perfect rest is not subject to agitation and being thrown off-center from itself.

Having discovered these *Gifts of God* a few years back in Lesson #122, and also being told I was "entrusted with them" (in Lesson #166), it dawned on me I needed to give them a lot more attention than I had been giving them to make them my "reality." As they stood in my present state, the *Gifts of God* somewhat eluded me. Why? My ego did not seem to be dismantled enough to allow them to take seed, sprout and grow. It was totally up to me to prepare my spiritual garden to receive them, and it was my responsibility to nurture them into qualities I brought into application.

The first thing I did was to make them into a laminated card with Jesus on one side, that I could carry around with myself. I have set this up, here in the book, so you can cut out the next page and laminate it. Then you can carry the *Gifts of God* with you wherever you go.

"The Gifts Of God"

1) Peace
2) Happiness
3) A Quiet Mind
4) A Certainty of Purpose
5) A Sense of Worth and Beauty That Transcends the World
6) Care
7) Safety
8) The Warmth of Sure Protection Always
9) A Quietness that Cannot Be Disturbed
10) A Gentleness that Never Can Be Hurt
11) A Deep Abiding Comfort
12) A Rest So Perfect It Can Never Be Upset

By having them laminated I could take the card with me anywhere, and in a moment of respite, look at the *Gifts of God* and ask myself where I stood with bringing them into application. After a while of doing this I had the 12 points memorized, and I could run through them in my mind anywhere. The question was always the same: am I embodying these *Gifts* in myself, or are they remaining as mere ideas, unrealized? Had I received the *Gifts of God* or was I just fooling myself?

What is needed for us to receive the *Gifts of God*? It seems like "knowing them" does not make much difference in our life. What is the Energy required in us to receive them, and bring them into application? Obviously "thought" cannot apply a truth. It can learn what it is, but then it constantly vacillates between the truth and its so-called "opposite." There is a determination beyond thinking in which an admission of helplessness at the thought level is necessary. With this admission, there is an invocation, a true prayer for the Help needed to bring Truth into application. I understand without the help of the Unknown, the Holy Spirit, I would not be able to access and maintain these holy *Gifts of God*. But with this help, I can. The Holy Spirit in me makes the application possible. This amounts to accessing the Strength of God in me: "God is the strength in which I trust." *ACIM*, Lesson #47

Peace—do I want this "above all else." Peace is the suspension of judgment, anger, discontent, wanting things to be "different." Can I do this? Do I want to drop my opinions? Can I give up blame, or projecting my problems onto others. I am 100% responsible for anything that is "non-peace." Peace is attainable when I want peace more than conflict. And I can agree with myself, my partner, my family, my work colleagues, to have a "conflict-free" relationship. "I could see peace instead of this," is Lesson #34 in *ACIM*. I can always decide for peace when I want to. Do I? Do you?

Happiness—this is not a fleeting joy. This is Constant Joy. The happiness of "letting all things be exactly as they are" is the beginning of finding happiness in all situations. (Lesson # 268) When I allow all things to be as is, I am content, and in a state of peace. I accept that Pure Joy is the nature of the universe, and if a situation is not reflecting this Pure Joy, then I am responsible to see it differently. I can shift my perception to see a forgiven world in which all my unhappiness is dissolved. Judgments are suspended for the truth, and truth goes hand in hand with Pure Joy. Without this surrender to the truth, I will continue to make sorrow and unhappiness real, in the sense that I justify them with "reasons." When I am willing to give up my "justifications" to prove my unhappiness, then I will be on the verge of Perfect Happiness being given to me. "God's will for me is perfect happiness," is Lesson #101 in *ACIM*.

A Quiet Mind—this is not as far-fetched or as complicated as it may seem. This does not require long hours of meditation and sitting in a yoga posture struggling to still the mind of its chatter. There is chatter. It is "normal." The question is what to do with it. Notice it. Do not "fight it." Observe it. There is a Quiet Mind and it is running in tandem with the chattering mind, the brain. The first thing to see is that the Quiet Mind is quiet even when the "chattering mind" is not. They are two different "minds." The Quiet Mind is there when you realize that it is not the mind of the brain or the mind of memory and thought. That is what we accumulate in our brain, in our various levels of consciousness, but the Quiet Mind exists transcendentally to this. It is *without thought* even in the midst of thought. When the lesson says, "My thoughts do not mean anything," Lesson #10, the mind of thought is left behind, and we see a glimpse of the Quiet Mind. It is that simple, requiring no effort. Just willingness to see the meaninglessness of thought itself.

A Certainty of Purpose—in this case, would my purpose be to liberate myself from all falseness, all sorrow, all conflict, all chatter of my incessant thought, all unhappiness? "Salvation is my only function here, " it says in Lesson #99, and then it says, "Salvation and Forgiveness are the same." Liberation and Salvation are the same as well. A Certainty of Purpose would be to put my Liberation in the first place. This includes putting Peace, Happiness, and a Quiet Mind in the first place as well. These are the attributes of my purpose, and I must be certain these are what I want "above all else."

A Sense of Worth and Beauty that Transcend the World—one can hardly fathom this kind of beauty, but it is there. When *ACIM* refers to the world, it means the thought-based world we made up—out of separation from our Source. The Source of our Worth is the very Beauty and Joy that exists independent of this world. Therefore when we transcend the world, we have a sense of this Worth and Beauty that defines our real Self. We have a sense of it.

Care—we all can have divine Care. As we were created, so shall we be maintained. The same benevolent and loving Creator Who created us would also be there to care for us. Even with bodies, our needs are met—we have the air to breathe, the water to drink, the food to eat, the light to see, and the space in which to exist. All is provided for us. So how could we ever say no one, or no Source "cares" for us? It is already given this absolute Care.

Safety—we could go on debating for a while how unsafe it is out there in the "concrete jungle" of the places we designed to live in. Safety is not in an external place. It is in a fearlessness we carry within ourselves. Can we be in an internal place in which fearlessness and Love are at the forefront of our awareness? "In fearlessness and Love, I spend today." This is Lesson #310. Who can do it? Are we willing to give it a go? In this state of mind, we can truly feel Safe.

A Quietness that Cannot Be Disturbed—we are not helpless with the aid of the Holy Spirit, which is the part of our mind that sees the truth of who we are as God created us. The Holy Spirit also sees the errors of the ego that keep us separated from this power of our true Identity. Looking past the one for the other, the true vision of the Holy Spirit will always silence our thought and put us in the Peace of Mind that cannot be disturbed. This invocation for the Holy Spirit's help is essential, though. It is the place in our mind that "knows," because it bypasses the place in our mind that "does not know" (but thinks that it does). The Holy Spirit brings the Quiet. It knows only the Quiet.

A Gentleness that Never Can Be Hurt—the person who can be gentle knows no fear. That is why gentleness makes sense. Gentleness is a natural giving-ness that sees the highest nature in the other person to whom one is gentle. Gentleness is not weakness, but rather it is Strength. The Strong can afford to be gentle. And the Strong know that it is the Strength of God that flows through them, and this Strength is limitless by nature, therefore Gentleness in Strength is limitless as well. Therefore, it can never be hurt.

A Deep Abiding Comfort—this is a constant gift. When one receives this gift one acknowledges the constancy of Joy. And Joy that is always around is very comforting. Comfort is of the Creator for the Created, which is all of us. God holds all Creation in the care and safety of its natural state of Being. In perfect harmony and balance, the entire Cosmos vibrates in the Comfort that is abiding. Reality is whole and complete, and Comfort is the realization of God's care for all of Creation. So I can relax. "God's will for me is perfect happiness," as stated in Lesson #101, and a deep abiding Comfort is the result of this Constant Care and Joy.

A Rest So Perfect It Can Never Be Disturbed—all of Creation is at rest in God. Rest is very dynamic. Universes spin and expand in an infinite unfolding of the Cosmos, yet even in this movement there is absolute Rest. What is at Rest is effortless. The Universe unfolds effortlessly. What has a nature to be, comes into being through an effortless action. When the bud is ready to burst there is no effort in that—and nothing can hold it back. It bursts into being by an action of rest. It is grounded in the very nature of itself, and it extends this Self in an instant of total Rest that cannot be disturbed.

The *Gifts of God* are deep, broad, and high at the same time. The ego-mind will *poo-poo* them as merely ephemeral moods and feelings, with not much value; yet the Mind of our Self will embrace them, explore them, apply them, and be ever grateful for the clarity of qualities embodied in them—leading us to be the Christ. To be the Christ is to accept the *Gifts of God.* To be the Christ is to embody the *Gifts of God.* To be the Christ is to share and extend the *Gifts of God*. To be the Christ is what we are here to be, and the *Gifts of God* make this Being possible.

10.
Love of Correction

The love of correction is the cornerstone of any spiritual evolution we make. Without it, there is no impetus for change, and no reason to look at ourselves in terms of evolution at all. Without it, we remain "victims" of circumstances and people beyond our control, or we become "control freaks" to keep our world in the dominant order we make up. Love of correction is always questioning ourselves, "what is in me" that has given me an experience or a result I don't want? What is the vibration in me in need of changing for me to have the experience of Joy and the *Gifts of God*?

During my seventeen years with my master teacher, Tara Singh, the *love of correction* was of paramount importance. Forgiveness, on which the foundation of *A Course in Miracles* teachings rest, and *love of correction,* emphasized by Tara Singh in his lectures and relationships, were virtually one and the same. What became apparent though, having a dynamic teacher in the flesh such as Tara Singh, one would be held accountable for this action to really take place in his life. Complacency and avoidance were unacceptable attitudes in the world around Tara Singh. Often we were put in the crucible of inner correction in which our egos were burnt to a crisp. This smelting of the inner metals of one's character was unavoidable, and without the love of correction, I would have been totally obliterated from the intensity of the fire surrounding the life lessons Tara Singh was dishing out.

There is a prayer in *ACIM* which Tara Singh felt was the equivalent of the "Lord's Prayer" in *ACIM* terms. It goes like this:

> *Forgive us our illusions, Father, and help us to accept our true relationship with You, in which there are no illusions, and where none can ever enter. Our holiness is Yours. What can there be in us that needs forgiveness when Yours is perfect? The sleep of forgetfulness is only the unwillingness to remember Your forgiveness and Your Love. Let us not wander into temptation, for the temptation of the Son of God is not Your Will. And let us receive only what You have given, and accept but this into the minds which You created and which You love. Amen.*
>
> *(ACIM; Text; Chapter 16; Section VII.)*

The love for correction lies in the giving up of illusions, yet, the difficulty is in seeing the illusions as illusions. We could have grievances and judgments that we deem justified, and these are the very illusions for which we need correction. The invocation for "forgiveness of illusions" in this prayer is at the crux of the love of correction. It begins by asking forgiveness for the errors our minds have made.

It is also in recognizing that there is a Power greater than our own to make the correction. Our main responsibility is to "admit the error"—to see our illusions. Then we ask for them to be released, *or corrected*. We are asking God to do this. We are asking to overcome our *unwillingness* to accept God's forgiveness and Love.

There is a Will of our Creator for us not to forget the perfection of our Self, and to not "wander into temptation" away from this perfection. What could be more clear? The love of correction culminates in the Help of the Holy Spirit to realign us in a direct relationship with our Creator. This is a very palpable and direct thing—not just a theory or a theological positioning. In fact, it is not theological at all. It is a correction of the right relationship with our Source in which we have certainty of purpose that this is the most important relationship of Life.

> *—help us to accept our true relationship with You, in which there are no illusions, and where none can ever enter.*

People do not usually think of their relationship with their Source of Life to be their primary relationship. Many do not even like to think of the word "God" anymore, as it has become so misused, racked with debilitating dogmas, and stripped of trust which should be its principal attribute. What would a "true relationship" with God be, *in which there are no illusions and none can ever enter?*

It is clear that *A Course in Miracles* re-establishes this primary relationship. And it does so with a direct but gentle means of inner correction. The Forgiveness and Love of God are for us to remember. We need to awaken from our self-imposed "sleep of forgetfulness." The love is there. The forgiveness is there—but we have forgotten it. How can we awaken from this dream of amnesia? Well, this awakening process is brought about by our *little willingness* to have the *love for correction.*

Truth will correct all errors in my mind.
(ACIM; Workbook; Lesson #107)

It is not only spoken about in the lessons of the *Course*, but it is made clear that correction is a major function of the truth in the minds of the students who undertake to master this curriculum. "Removing the blocks to the awareness of Love's presence," is the purpose spoken about in the Introduction to the Text—and it is this *removing of the blocks* that is another way of saying *inner correction*. The errors in my mind will be removed by truth, an act of correction that merits my love.

Miracles are seen in the light of this inner correction, which we could also call forgiveness. Forgiveness is at the core of the process, but even deeper than we may think. First I always have to see that forgiveness is for my self—always. Even if it is someone else who seems to perpetrate the mistake, it is I who must ask, "What is in me that has attracted this mistake in my life." There is no separate error. All errors are made and corrected in my own mind, therefore I am 100% responsible even for what I witness, though I may not be an "active player" in the drama before me. The fact I am seeing the drama makes me the one who can apply the most reparative force—my love of correction would be the most transformative action I could offer any situation run amuck. This does not require even my involvement in the events. It does require, though, that I see my thoughts contributing to the problem and be willing to have them be admitted, corrected and transmuted.

Love of truth, love of correction, love of my brothers, love of God are all one. Love is a state of being in which all problems have been solved, and everything is complete, and nothing needs to be added nor subtracted from what is. Separation from my Source has been undone. In fact, I see that I never was separated from my Source. I could not live without this Divine Connection, and for me to exist at all this Connection was always so, always fully intact, and separation was just an "illusion of despair." "Let me recognize my problems have been solved." This is *ACIM* Lesson # 80. The only "problem" was separation from my Source, and this could only be "imagined." In reality, I could never be separated from my Source, therefore the problems this error would have made are now gone. They are illusions from which I have awakened.

PART 3

The Second Coming

11. Life Purpose

One of the ultimate questions of Life is "Why am I here?" What is my purpose here on earth, in this incarnation, in this Life I share with God and with all living things? For the most part, people are confined to families, careers, and hobbies. The larger questions may go overlooked. For many the issues of survival take up all their attention. For others more affluent, the questions of entrepreneurship may preoccupy their aspirations for success. "What am I contributing to the Whole of Life?" is a deeper question that the seers and visionaries of humanity pose to themselves. This is a question of purpose. It transcends all other questions and gives us meaning beyond the measures of conventions and expectations of our world.

When my teacher Tara Singh came to the United States from India in the early 1950s he was fortunate to have come from privilege. Much of his life had been spent in "Divine Leisure," as he called it. People would ask him, "What do you do for a living?" He had not seen his life in that way. It was a question that misplaced the very purpose of life itself. It was like saying, "What do you do to survive?" A crude question, he had always been cared for by the grace of life, by the affluence of his family, and by the meetings he had with eminent beings like Gandhi, Nehru, and Mrs. Roosevelt, among others. For him to think in terms of, "What do you do for a living?" was an affront to his Life Purpose. His purpose was to make contact with the Divine Truth, to be ever grateful for the elements that sustained him, and to be open to receive the blessings of a benevolent Creator at work in the very crux of his everyday affairs.

A life purpose is one I share with God. The ultimate Forces of Life guide me when I am with my true Life Purpose. Gratitude is due to these Forces, and they are not mysterious. The simplest of these are the elements themselves—fire, air, water, earth, and space. Do I allow my very breath to guide me? The Purpose of Life is to contribute to the Peace and Joy of a Reality which is already there. I make contact with my Source, and my Purpose is to be consistent with the Will of this Source. The Will would always be some greater expression of Love, or Truth, of Goodness which serves the whole. This co-creation would use my talents and interests.

Whatever I am doing to fulfill my Life Purpose would increase my Peace and Joy. For me, the creative arts are essential in my pursuit to be productive and feel good. I use my talents to express the natural beauty I see all around me. These expressions are for others to ponder and observe—and in this exchange, my Joy is shared. This sharing is my Life Purpose. A tree shares its Being with the world—its wood, oxygen, shade, a shelter for animals, compost, presence, and beauty, etc. A human shares his communion with Divine Forces that others may connect with Love as well.

A Life Purpose gives meaning to my time on earth. Meaning is Love in this dimension. This is the most important focus any human being can have. The purpose of life is to Love and be Loved. It may sound too general, too broad, yet if this one purpose is mastered first and foremost, then it is applied to all other areas of life—which make them part of the purpose. Love of life is transferable to Love of Self, Love of a partner, Love of work, Love of family, Love of neighbors, etc. Without this primary purpose, the meaning of everything is subject to change and conflict. This is why the discovery of our Life Purpose is so essential. Once it is mastered the whole of life is one of Pure Joy.

Relationships are elevated into the Divine vibrations that make up our "heaven on earth." This transformation is only possible with the mastery of Love—our main purpose for Being. The simplicity of this purpose is what gives it power. Everyone can master it—no matter where they are in their personal life. It does not depend on socio-economic status. All humans can master a Life Purpose equally. Love is the purpose, and all people can access this when they are willing and determined to do so.

I have a function God would have me fill.
(ACIM; Workbook; Lesson #192)

Did we ever stop to think about what God would want us to do here? Is that kind of a question even relevant in our lives? What is this function spoken about in Lesson #192?

> *It is your Father's holy Will that you complete Himself, and that your Self shall be His sacred Son, forever pure as He, of love created and in love preserved, extending love, creating in its name, forever one with God and with your Self. Yet what can such a function mean within a world of envy, hatred and attack?*
>
> *Therefore, you have a function in the world in its own terms. For who can understand a language far beyond his simple grasp? Forgiveness represents your function here. It is not God's creation, for it is the means by which untruth can be undone. And who would pardon Heaven? Yet on earth, you need the means to let illusions go. Creation merely waits for your return to be acknowledged, not to be complete.*

This function God would have us fill is to be our true Self. This Self is wholly loving, joyous, giving, living and extending a state of grace, fully alive and helpful, productive and at peace with itself. The function God would have us fill is to bring a version of heaven to earth. This should be everyone's primary goal—to create in their own actual life perfect happiness that is contagious to those around them.

But OK, often we do not find ourselves doing too well in creating this "heaven on earth." So what is our function amidst those struggles and turmoil?

Forgiveness represents your function here.

We need to explore the true meaning of forgiveness. What is it (in terms of a restorative function) we all must master? There is a "forgiveness" of the ego that says, "So and so did something bad, but because I am so good and charitable, I can let him off the hook." This is not the forgiveness the Christ is talking about in the *Course.* Self-examination is always required. The inner correction is always asking, "What is in me that attracted this event in my life? What is my part in this scenario?" This needs to be applied to anything that is not pure joy and happiness in our lives.

Certainly, we know by now, the wise from immemorial have given us the edict, "Know Thyself." As much as 2500 years ago, it was chiseled above the entrance to the Temple in Delphi, Greece. And here we have the same challenge in this age as all human beings do. "Who am I?" "Why am I here?" "What am I to do with this life?" Life purpose is paramount in our discoveries. The functions of letting go which forgiveness implies, a kind of all-pervasive absolution from any consequences of mistakes, is a mighty function. And we need the Christ to do it, as He is the master of this Life Action.

A Course in Miracles calls this *complete forgiveness* the Atonement. And makes very clear that the Christ is in charge of it:

> *I am in charge of the process of Atonement, which I undertook to begin. When you offer a miracle to any of my brothers, you do it to* yourself *and me. The reason you come before me is that I do not need miracles for my own Atonement, but I stand at the end in case you fail temporarily. My part in the Atonement is the cancelling out of all errors that you could not otherwise correct. When you have been restored to the recognition of your original state, you naturally become part of the Atonement yourself. As you share my unwillingness to accept error in yourself and others, you must join the great crusade to correct it; listen to my voice, learn to undo error and act to correct it.* ***The power to work miracles belongs to you. I will provide the opportunities to do them, but you must be ready and willing.*** *Doing them will bring conviction in the ability, because conviction comes through accomplishment. The ability is the potential, the achievement is its expression, and the Atonement, which is the natural profession of the children of God, is the purpose.*
>
> *(ACIM; Text; Chapter 1; Section III.)*

I apologize for my extensive quotations here from *A Course in Miracles,* but these passages are so important—so revealing of our true purpose here—that I cannot put them in any less of an inclusion. They are passages that would behoove us to read over and over again until they are instilled in our blood and bones. The beauty of their clarity and melodious sound of truth beyond our normal thought is unsurpassed.

> ***The power to work miracles belongs to you. I will provide the opportunities to do them, but you must be ready and willing.***

Are we ready to work miracles? Are we willing to allow the Christ to provide us with these opportunities to see things differently, and join in this "great crusade" to correct all inner "errors" in ourselves? Will we accept our role in the Atonement?

Our Life Purpose is not obscure. It is made very clear. The Second Coming of the Christ is already in us as the realization of this purpose. How could we miss it, except by our unwillingness to take it up, and substitute some other "minor purpose" we think is more important than our major one?

I would like to conclude this chapter with a prayer of unfathomable beauty and grace. It gives us the whole purpose of life that can be applied to any of the other endeavors we undertake. If we are engineers or teachers or bus drivers; or heads of corporations or public servants in governments; or cleaning ladies or entrepreneurs, small business owners or retired elderly; students in school or students of life already engaged in our profession—the Life Purpose which is the highest and the most rewarding is stated here:

I am here only to be truly helpful.
I am here to represent Him Who sent me.
I do not have to worry about what to say or what to do, because He Who sent me will direct me.
I am content to be wherever He wishes, knowing He goes there with me.
I will be healed as I let Him teach me to heal.

(ACIM; Text; Chapter 2; Section V)

Can we represent the highest part of our Self? This is the Christ. He or She is not separate from who we are. The *Second Coming* is our awakening into that, through total forgiveness, into this Self God created as us!

The purpose of life is to be the Christ Self we are, and He is there to help us. "Know Thyself" is the purpose that is synonymous with "Know the Christ in us." As I said, it does not matter where you find yourself in life right now; it can be applied to any situation, profession, relationship, challenge, or inspiration by which you are grounded and guided.

The purpose of Life is to know our Self of absolute Love—Love of Self through Love of our Brothers and Sisters, our planet, our "enemies," our Life on earth. It is the Love of God we say we may want to realize, yet still must take up the directions, forgiveness, and willingness to fulfill.

12.
Living as the Christ

Who do we hold in reverence and even high regard? Who are the people who shaped our lives and inspired us to be a better person? Who are our heroes holding the standard of excellence to whom we aspire? Everyone has some example of a torchbearer in their life who holds up the light of clear direction—one who illuminates a pathway to action which shapes our life and determines our overall fate. Who is that for you?

As an artist, of course, I had my heroic figures in the field of art history—and their paintings—Leonardo's "Woman with Ermine," Grunewald's "Isenheim Altarpiece," Vermeer's "Artist in His Studio," Picasso's "Drawing of Stravinsky," Matisse's "Red Room," among others. As far as literary figures who loomed largely, Thoreau, Emerson and Whitman in the New World; D.H. Lawrence and Dostoyevsky in the Old World.

Brought up in the Methodist Church, primarily under my mother's influence, I gained an appreciation for Jesus. Sometimes I wonder though, being a very visual person if it was the church spectacle and beauty of the materials and architecture that drew me in on this one. When I came of age to declare myself in the Methodist faith, I opted out. It seemed like such a limitation to declare myself anything, separating me off from the rest of a vast ocean of possibilities that could not be contained by any organizational confinement. I knew even then, around the age of 13 or so, that organized religion was not my thing. I quietly renounced the whole *church tradition* and proceeded to get myself to art school in the passion of my choice—painting, and drawing, which were my major forms of spiritual inquiry.

However, after graduate school in Philadelphia and seven years of academic life in the world of art, I was still searching for the answer in matters of the spirit. Art is an encounter with Life and the synthesis of that encounter into some medium of expression. Yet the bigger questions remained, and these were questions that went beyond my reservoir of aesthetic knowledge. They stood outside of the physical realms of my former study and entered into realms of the metaphysical questions. It was not until I met up with Rebirthing and Sondra Ray that these questions started to make sense. In meeting her, I began to see that thought always precedes results or manifestations. Therefore to have dominion over my world, I would have to examine and gain dominion over my thoughts—which is to say, become well trained in the cause and effects of the mind.

Not too far into my involvement with Rebirthing—a conscious connected breathing process that allows one to access the subconscious thoughts one has, all the way back to birth—I took a training with Sondra Ray called "The Loving Relationships Training." It opened my eyes in revolutionary ways. The main epiphany came in the form of a statement Sondra made about a book called *A Course in Miracles*. She said, "This is the most important book written in 2000 years." Well, that got my attention. I went out and bought the books immediately, as at the time *ACIM* was published in three volumes: Text, Workbook for Students, and Manual for

Teachers. Little did I know at the time this would change the course of my life, and put me in touch with my bigger destiny.

For those of us who have been familiar with *ACIM* for decades, studying its lessons and principles, it is not a surprise, nor too farfetched a statement to say, "This *is* the most important book written in 2000 years." Nor is it inaccurate to say that it is authored by the Christ. I will not go into the story of its origins here, but just to mention for those who may be unfamiliar with its history, it was scribed by a clinical psychologist in New York City from approximately 1966-1976. Her name, Dr. Helen Schucman, is destined to be among the names of great scribes from whom we have received the holiest of scriptures from the beginning of humankind's recording of sacred and divine revelations. This is her contribution, here in the Western World, of the paramount truths recorded for uplifting any person willing to go into realms of the Absolute. She heard a voice from Jesus, and she wrote down what He was saying. We have this now as *A Course in Miracles,* a thought system of Absolute Knowledge.

For me, receiving this Absolute Knowledge was a way of restoring my relationship with Jesus, my childhood Master Teacher. It was a way of *not throwing the baby out with the bathwater,* as the saying goes. I could have a direct relationship with the Christ without the interference of an organized religion that adhered to any false religious theology which came along with it. Furthermore, the language of *A Course in Miracles* was different than that of the *Bible*—in that Jesus seemed to be speaking directly to me, in the present time, not to some Middle Eastern character walking around in robes in the desert, from a very distant past. The Christ was here for me in a language I could understand and take in—and this turned out to be a blessing beyond my wildest imagination that was possible.

I was introduced into *A Course in Miracles* around 1985. By 1987 I was studying the work seriously, going through the Text and the Lessons in the Workbook in a disciplined manner. But it was not until 1989 I blundered into a lecture on a cassette tape titled *Bringing A Course in Miracles Into Application*. I heard for the first time Tara Singh, who became my teacher of *A Course in Miracles* for 17 years. Tara Singh had been groomed by Dr. Schucman to give lectures on the *Course* around the country. By 1989 he had been doing this for over six years, and he had a non-profit educational foundation in Los Angeles that served as a school and a disseminator of books, tapes, workshops on this modern-day scripture. Mr. Singh was the dynamic teacher who awakened students to the truth imparted by the Christ Consciousness outlined in the *Course*. I developed a close relationship with him.

For two-and-a-half years Tara Singh had spoken with Dr. Schucman every day at the same time. It is she who brought him to the stillness of the peace of God discussed in the Lessons of the Workbook. She also made it clear to him, "*A Course in Miracles* is not to be learned, it is to be lived." In other words, intellectual understanding is not enough for any transformation to take place in the student—he or she must live the words for the *Course* to have any meaning at all. We are too addicted to intellectual knowledge without making the demands of the application, especially when it comes to lofty spiritual principles. The practice is the key. Application is the essential ingredient to the work of *ACIM*. Living as the Christ is our responsibility as a student of this dynamic book. In fact, the book is not just a book, in the end. It is the Christ Himself in the form of true words being spoken to us, His students. The only real question, then, is—do we have the ears to hear them and apply them?

Tara Singh made it clear that we can easily deceive ourselves in thinking that we are in an elevated state of being, when in fact we have not removed the blocks in us that prevent our application. He talked about the realization of true words. Most of us have entanglements, problems, attachments, and various internal impurities that still need to be addressed to rise to the level of the Christ. This is the "spiritual practice" we all must go through to purify ourselves and *remove the blocks to the awareness of love's presence. (Introduction, Text, ACIM)* This is an arduous process of "undoing" and bringing order to our life. Yet, this is where Jesus Himself begins with the lessons of the Workbook: "Nothing I see means anything," is Lesson #1. This is a direct affront to our ego, which has spent a lifetime giving meaning to the people, places and things in our world. Now, with one fell swoop, that world is being dismantled and turned upside down. Who is willing to go through this dismantling—this undoing process, in reality? It is not for the faint of heart.

Living as the Christ begins with undoing a life of "not living as the Christ." This may feel very humbling because it is. Most of us, even having gone to Church and been brought up as so-called "Christians," have not necessarily lived as the Christ. We have held this Character as a kind of heroic figure on a pedestal of unreachable proportions, Who sometimes makes us feel better in times of duress and incidents in which we made mistakes. But to *Live as the Christ* was not even mentioned as a possible role model for structuring our goals and long term plans. We were taught some kind of skill to fit into the practical professions of the modern world—be an engineer, an accountant, or perhaps a doctor or a lawyer. But to be the Christ—wow—are you nuts? The cell in a mental institution would be more like your next residence than a classroom at a mystery school. Mystery schools hardly exist in the West. They barely exist at all, anywhere.

A Course in Miracles is this school. Finally, we have one that addresses the inner issues of human yearning. And we need not even leave our house to be in this school. It is here to fulfill our deepest and broadest yearning. We yearn to know our higher Self, and this work we are given to do in *ACIM* can awaken that awareness in us. In a set of Lessons that we undertake to read and practice for a year—one a day for 365 days—we are given exercises that will transform our inner outlook of who we are as God created us. Of course, this will be very confronting to our ego, because this other "self we made up" is the problem of *living as the Christ.* We usually don't want to let go of it. It is "not practical" to do so.

However, in our practical world, we have judgments, opinions, desires, goals, and relationships that may not serve us in living as the Christ. And, we have a great reluctance to change what He may ask us to give up—something which could prove a block to living a higher life. We may have a sense of security, or dominance, or advantage that would be threatened if we were to consider living as the Christ. Many of the things we value may not be so valuable in this other world of Christ Consciousness. We may not even value this lifestyle in the end, for fear that we would have to sacrifice or give up something we have worked so hard to acquire. We may want to live as the Christ, but also want to keep the self we made up as our "red badge of courage" that rewards us for all the hard work we put into making our personality in the world.

I am the holy Son of God Himself.
(ACIM; Workbook; Lesson # 191)

What would most of us do with this statement? It is a statement of Identity. Any "I AM" statement tells us who we are. As a Son of God, what would that do to our sense of Self? In our organized church we were too often told Jesus was the "only Son of God," sent to save us from being irretrievable sinners. He "died for our sins" and took on our negatives so we could be saved by His pure and forgiving Love. Well, this ends up making us feel bad that a totally innocent man had to die so we could be redeemed from going straight to hell. What a bunch of baloney. No wonder we all wanted to leave the church behind with that kind of self-condemning logic.

Jesus clears up this false theology by stating in the Text of *A Course in Miracles* the proper view of our relationship with

Him. He refers to Himself as an "elder brother" for whom we should not be in awe, but rather respect:

> *Equals should not be in awe of one another because awe implies inequality. It is therefore an inappropriate reaction to me. An elder brother is entitled to respect for his greater experience, and obedience for his greater wisdom. He is also entitled to love because he is a brother, and to devotion if he is devoted. It is only my devotion that entitles me to yours. There is nothing about me that you cannot attain. I have nothing that does not come from God. The difference between us now is that I have nothing else. This leaves me in a state which is only potential in you.*
>
> *(ACIM; Text; Chapter 1; Section II; ¶ 3)*

"Equals should not be in awe of one another." How would this affect our relationship with the Christ Whom we placed as an object of worship in our churches? Respect among equals is a lot different than having Jesus as "the only Son of God," in which case we become so much "less than." Granted, He does state that our relationships have other stuff in them, implying stuff "not of God," and therefore without miracles we would remain only in the potential of being the Christ, not the actuality. This is why He gives us *A Course in Miracles*—which amounts to a *Course* of inner correction.

There is a clarity of correction in the words of this modern-day scripture. They are the words of the Christ to you who are reading them, and this is very direct. If you imagined Christ sitting in a chair across from you, and you were having a conversation with Him, this is what *A Course in Miracles* is—a direct talk you are having with Jesus, your "elder brother." He is giving you the clarity of Your eternal being through this conversation, and every word you read is right out of His mouth. There is no priest, no hierarchy of church organization between you and the Christ. He is awakening you directly every time you open this *Course* and every time you go to this font of pure and living water of truth.

Mistakes have been made, and we know that. But a mistake can be corrected without the heavily laden guilt that comes with the word "sin." We were created in a state of grace, of innocence, of everlasting joy. We forgot who we were in this Divine Being, but this was a mistake, not a sin. The truth is our original innocence, not our "original sin" (as the church would have us believe) is the basis of our Being. God created us sinless. This is the real fact. And the function of the Christ is to help us remember that fact. We can borrow His certainty to come to this realization of our true Identity. We are the younger brothers and sisters of the Christ Who helps us to wake up to our God created Self.

The Son of God is My Identity.
(ACIM; Workbook; Lesson #252)

We spend a lifetime making up a self with whom we identify. I am Markus Ray, an author, an artist, a husband, a son, a brother, a teacher, a this or a that. And in this personal identification exist all my doubts, insecurities, shame, regrets, problems, memories of things gone awry, etc. Did I ever once think of myself as the *Son of God*? And if I did identify with this Son of God, with whom would I be walking on this road of Life? The implication is that I would be walking with the Christ, I would be Living as the Christ.

A Course in Miracles is our opportunity to do that. Having a relationship with its true words is having a relationship with the Christ. *The Second Coming* is merely the acceptance that this relationship is here and now, and it is already taking place within you. The means are given. Every person has this opportunity to *live as the Christ* in their study and application of *ACIM*. It is His gift that was promised and delivered. Christ has come again in you who are the "Holy Son of God Himself," as made clear through this "most important book written in 2000 years."

13. Rebooting Our Life

In good computer practices when you come to an impasse in a program that makes it malfunction, the first thing you try to fix it is to shut down and reboot your whole system, and in this resetting, you will probably restore the program to its original state—and things miraculously begin to work again due to this simple stopping and restarting action. Miracles are kind of like a reboot. We reach an impasse in our life in which we do not have the solution, and nothing we have tried works, and nothing we do makes things better—instead, the things we tried may have made matters worse. We are somewhat at the end of our rope, and the only thing we can do is surrender to a Higher Force, admit we don't know what the heck we are doing, and pray to a benevolent Creator that our mistakes will be absolved and order will be restored.

A Course in Miracles is this very *reboot*. Just when it seems matters could get no worse, there is a spark of hope that shines through the events in our life that lead us out of the quagmire of problems. It begins with the advent of forgiveness in our life, and this forgiveness is mainly one in which we take 100% responsibility for everything that happens in our field of experience. This responsibility is the beginning of true forgiveness. It is the "key to happiness" of which Jesus speaks:

Forgiveness is the key to happiness.
Forgiveness offers everything I want.
(ACIM; Workbook; Lessons #121 & #122)

The forgiveness here is a responsibility for sight. What we are observing in our experience is a result of our mental and emotional field, and this field is composed of thoughts and feelings that are in us *before* attracting the experience to us. This is basic metaphysical truth: thoughts precede manifestations.

> *This is the only thing that you need do for vision, happiness, release from pain and the complete escape from sin, all to be given you. Say only this, but mean it with no reservations, for here the power of salvation lies:*
>
> ***I** am **responsible for what I see.***
> ***I choose the feelings I experience, and I decide upon the goal I would achieve.***
> ***And everything that seems to happen to me I ask for, and receive as I have asked.***
>
> *(ACIM; Text; Chapter 21; Section II; ¶ 2)*

I would say this is a reboot. It is a total turning off of the system of our judgments and our thoughts of management. It is an admission that "I am the cause" of all my problems. No one else. And because I am taking 100% responsibility for everything, the invocation for correction is in my hands, and I can make this appeal to Truth to help me restore harmony to any situation. In these statements is true forgiveness. True forgiveness is the total "reboot" of my life, that will restore the proper functioning of my life to me. Grace is given to those who see that the errors are in themselves to correct. And because of this foremost responsibility, they no longer blame others for their "outcomes."

There is a moment of suspended animation, it seems, when we are shown that we are the makers of all of our perceptions and feelings—and there is nothing outside of us that is "beyond our control." What we think and feel inside us forms the pre-existing vibrational field that calls in its corresponding experience. The external is just a demonstration of our internal programming. So what would it be like to awaken to God's original program placed in us, before we added our viruses and stuff to that Divine Order in our Life? Miracles are actions of cleaning out the malware and viruses of wrong thinking that have infiltrated our thought system. Miracles are corrective devices that reboot our life. And the biggest reboot is offered in the first ten lessons of *A Course in Miracles*.

Nothing I see means anything.
(ACIM; Workbook; Lesson #1)

Why is that? Why has all the meaning I have given to the people, places, things, and experiences of my life amounted to the "meaningless?" There are two thought systems which seem to do battle in my process to awaken. The self I *made up* opposes the Self God created in its imagined separation from its Source. God's Peace and Joy are offered me but I must first empty myself of the programs I have running, and reset my mind to the original defaults God put there.

For most of us, this is not all that easy to accept the fact that our perception is off, and we have to relinquish it first before we can be shown a new one. We are attached to the past; we do not want to give up what we have made and experienced, even if it is less than desirable. We are caught in the repetition of memory, even if those memories are replaying as pain and suffering.

My thoughts do not mean anything.
(ACIM; Workbook; Lesson #10)

In this "process of Atonement" that Jesus lays out in the Lessons of *A Course in Miracles*, it is important to realize there is total retraining of the mind which He undertakes to do with us. Are we willing to walk along with Him in this undoing process? This is only possible if we are willing to *reboot our minds*, which amounts to shutting them down totally before we push the restart button.

This shutting down has profound effects. And in order to do it we really have to get this point about taking 100% responsibility for all thoughts, feelings, and experiences that occur in our Life. Without this 100% responsibility for *everything that seems to happen to me,* I would remain a victim of circumstances "beyond my control." This victimhood is a false assessment of cause. Causes for things that go wrong are negative and fearful thoughts, memories and feelings already in my mind that has not been forgiven—or transmuted with Divine Correction—and so they repeat themselves in the present as the results I don't want. Errors are just unforgiven thoughts. A mind full of these is a "victim." And victimhood is always in error.

I am not the victim of the world I see.
(ACIM; Workbook; Lesson #31)

The "world" is just a print out of my programming. And if it is showing me something painful, then that faulty programming of pain is in me, and I have the responsibility to correct it. I can correct it with the help of the Holy Spirit.

What does this "help" look like? One cannot say the Holy Spirit is a sensory thing. It is not a "knowable" thing either, apart from its relationship to the miraculous happenings we can observe as its results. The instant you try to define it, like God, you would be limiting its scope. It is best described as a force of Absolute Love that can restore what fell out of Love back to its original Nature, in Love. The Holy Spirit is the medium of miracles. It is a great and benevolent Unknown Force that acts in our Favor to restore to our awareness to the Grandeur of God of which we are a part. The Holy Spirit is the active energy of the Christ. Christ can direct the Holy Spirit at His Will to help us because His Will and God's are ONE. Therefore, He is "tapped in, tuned in and turned on," as Esther Hicks would say, to His universal Life Force that makes His Power unlimited. Now it is used in the Service to humanity to awaken them to Absolute Love. What could be better?

But the reboot is necessary before we can get the good stuff. Our minds are full of beliefs that divide us, limitations that hold us back, and grievances that create friction and conflict in our relationships. All this has to be erased before we can step into the Absolute of Unconditional Love and Pure Joy. These misperceptions of thought fill our minds with problems and fears, the exact opposite of Love—the "problem-free state of being." Krishnamurti, and his student Tara Singh, my teacher, stressed coming to a "Still and Silent Mind." Thought itself cannot be trusted to put us in the realm of Truth, in actuality. It can only manufacture a "substitute" that fools us for a moment but does not liberate us from our inner turmoil. Only the ending of thought can get us in touch with the Absolute. Five seconds of that Silence are worth a whole life. And in my experience, one needs a direct relationship with a Spiritual Master to come to this inner Peace. The true teacher, or the "sadguru," helps the student reboot his mind in the "Stillness of the Peace of God." He does this by pointing out all the falseness hidden in the student, and by helping him to clean it up with an extended period of inner correction. The Teacher also observes the errors within himself and transmutes them to silence as well.

The real Teacher helps us reboot. The female saint Amritanadamayi, commonly called Amma, travels around the world giving millions of people hugs. Having Her darshan, placing our being in Her Holy Presence, brings a total reboot of our minds. Her energy field amidst this embrace brings a person's mind to total silence. This blessing is unforgettable.

What is She doing when She hugs you? She has certainly absorbed Herself in a state of Divine Love, yet She can also bring other people into that forcefield of the Absolute too, so they also feel this enveloping of Divine and Absolute Love. She is a Master, she is a channel of the Christ. Christ is not a "personality" in this case. Jesus the man channeled the Christ, as he was 100% in touch with His Divine Identity as the Son of God. Amma is channeling the Christ in Her version. Total absorption into Her Divine Connection, she lives in the state of the miraculous all of the time. There is no time she is a personality. She is an embodiment of the Divine Mother Herself. Just as Jesus was an embodiment of the Son of God. Both had "rebooted" their minds so they could receive a new Mind of God, free of all limitations—

> ***At one with every aspect of creation, and limitless in power and in peace.*** *(ACIM; Workbook; Lesson #95)*

14. Stepping Out of Fear

Jesus makes things very clear in *A Course in Miracles* that we have a decision to make. There is a distinct difference, which is essential we understand, between the "two selves" available to us. The "self we made up" (in separation from awareness of our Source) He calls the ego. The Self God created (which He represents in total awareness of that union) He calls the Christ. The *self we made up* has fear as its domain, with a kind of manufactured veneer we call a "better life," which is only a skin-deep appearance. We feel separated from our Source of Peace and Joy. We vacillate between the veneer and the fear underneath, because our minds are split in duality. This confusion results in death in the end. The basis of the ego is fear and separation. And this whole complex of fear that leads eventually to death is the "descent into hell."

The Self God created has Heaven as its domain. Its basis is Love. It is Whole and One. It doesn't vacillate between two different states of opposites—Joy or sorrow—as it has sided with the One. It is in a state of Peace and Joy and nothing else. What is not Peace and Joy in our world is to be forgiven—transmuted with miracles. The result of this transmutation to Wholeness is Immortal Life with no end. And this begins in the Mind identified with the Spirit. The Body is "a wholly neutral thing," (ACIM, Lesson #294) in this view. The body's very neutrality keeps it functioning as the "teaching device" of the Mind—used to communicate only Love. We can keep the body as long as we have a use for it—in serving our brothers and demonstrating that they are Love as well.

Heaven or Hell? Love or Fear? Life or Death? The choice seems like it ought to be a simple one. Well, it is, but the unwillingness of the ego makes it complicated. At the base of the "self we made up" is tremendous resistance to relinquish the past—full of struggles, triumphs, and defeats—that seem to *define us*. We are conditioned by the known. What we "know" is touted as the great erudite bastion of self-identity we fought hard to construct and make up. The more we know the more expert we can be, and the more domination we can exert over life and the gyrations we all go through to make ourselves a better personal self. We are obsessed with "self-improvement," because deep down in ourselves we do not have the Love and esteem commensurate with the Cosmic Forces that created the Universe. Why not?

We are of that Cosmic Creation—that Divine Extension of Self-Identity. Somehow, somewhere, for some unknown reason, we separated from this Self God Created and made up our paltry versions of a personality racked with fear and distrust, dissatisfaction and debilitating denial of the Gloriousness we truly are. We have found ourselves more often than we would like to admit, in our own personal "polite hell." Or maybe not so polite.

We have another chance. We can consolidate our energy to make a decision. Jesus makes very clear to us in His lessons that we must choose between the self we made up and the Self God created—a decision right now for us to ponder and make:

Heaven is the decision I must make.
(ACIM; Workbook; Lesson #138)

and,

The power of decision is my own.
(ACIM; Workbook; Lesson #152)

What is this decision that would plummet me into another realm of the Joy of God in this dimension? This decision is to be made NOW, in this physical body, in this circumstance in which I find myself, in this time and place of the visceral reality of physicality. Heaven on Earth is not only the goal, but the promise and the legacy left to us by Jesus for us to accept. And it will be made up of the same "stuff" in which we find ourselves now. Truly there is a shift in consciousness awaiting us in which the very thing or relationship we saw as Hell before is translated anew into Heaven. This is nothing short of a new perception of the *real world:*

> *This is a very simple course. Perhaps you do not feel you need a course which, in the end, teaches that only reality is true. But do you believe it? When you perceive the real world, you will recognize that you did not believe it. Yet the swiftness with which your new and only real perception will be translated into knowledge will leave you but an instant to realize that this alone is true. And then everything you made will be forgotten; the good and the bad, the false and the true. For as Heaven and earth become one, even the real world will vanish from your sight. The end of the world is not its destruction, but its translation into Heaven. The reinterpretation of the world is the transfer of all perception to knowledge. (ACIM; Text; Chapter 11; Section VIII.)*

This is stepping out of fear. "There is nothing to fear," Jesus tells us in Lesson #48. Are we going to accept that? It is essential in our "reinterpretation of the world." The *real world* is not some perfected corner of the universe in which we have all the particular conditions just so to our liking, requiring us to *stand guard* over it. The real world has no resemblance to our own doing at all. It is a state of mind and being that has *completely let go* of any attachments of the senses. It is a kind of suspended animation in which we are still "in a body" and the realm of physicality, but we are identified with a wave of peace and joy that cannot ever be affected by external conditions. Now, for the most part, shifting conditions freak us out; but when the perception of reality is "transferred to knowledge," truly, "There is nothing to fear."

Who has done this? It is a challenge. Our life is a workshop for us to transcend fear. Our life is an opportunity for us to embrace Love as the basis of our being, more than the limited scope of it we may have at the moment. There is always ascension up the scale of our evolutionary awakening here. Yet, there is also a transmutation which does not take time and space to have. The miracle is a shift outside the realm of time that puts us in the timeless. It is a sudden shift into another quality of awareness in which fear has been abolished. We are no longer thinking in terms of what could happen badly to us, what could "go wrong," what catastrophe could befall us, or what temporal attachment would turn to dust. We are stepping out of fear for a good reason—to be our true and God created Self. This is a joy of the spirit into which we enter. And it is very palpable in the end—the translation of our world *into Heaven*.

We could do an exercise—what is your biggest fear? Make a list of them. Be honest. Fear of lack? Fear of relationships ending? Fear of disapproval at work? Fear of loneliness? Fear you won't accomplish your dreams? Fear of people? Fear of being exposed? People have a lot of fears. But it is important to see that they all are the same fear—fear is a diversion from Love. Fear is a diversion from the certainty of Divine Providence. Fear is a "disconnect" from our Source. We cannot be disconnected from our Source, but we "think" we can be. Thought and fear are nearly synonymous. This is why Jesus, and Krishnamurti as well, make it clear that we have to step out of thought itself to be free of fear—fear is thought. Fear, in the eyes of God, is meaningless. And the thought which composes the fear is meaningless as well:

My thoughts do not mean anything.
(ACIM; Workbook; Lesson #10)
and
A meaningless world engenders fear.
(ACIM; Workbook; Lesson #13)

What is meant by a "meaningless world?" A meaningless world is one that has uncertainty and fear as its basis. Fear of attack and counter-attack too often hold relationships in place. "I don't feel love for you, but I fear my life without you, so you get to be special." Specialness is the basis for fear-based relationships. But specialness is not Love, because it is too often a cover-up for a deep-seated fear. Stepping out of fear is also stepping out of specialness.

A Course in Miracles gives us a roadmap out of fear. With a serious dedication to doing the 365 Lessons exactly as prescribed, I guarantee you will step more out of fear and place yourself in the vibrations of Absolute Love. Your higher-Self begins to dawn in your mind, and Peace and Joy will be your inheritance for this gift of One Year. The inner work you do on yourself will take a certain amount of self-discipline, but you can do it.

Without getting into too many personal details, I can say that my life before getting together with Sondra Ray had a lot of fear in it. Tara Singh, my teacher of *A Course in Miracles* for many years, was my guide and mentor. But he took a very "hands-off" approach when it came to me working out issues in my everyday life. He would not interfere with the dynamics and entanglements I already had in place. That was my job. The work of undoing was my responsibility within the very life I had made up. It would have to be like this. A true teacher does not interfere with the status quo; he does affect it though, with the light of a higher reason he awakens in the student. He points the way, but the student must take the steps himself to go along that *way*. The *proof* of whether the student has the ears to hear the teachings is how he will transform his life. The workshop becomes life itself then. Life is the proof.

After Tara Singh passed on April 7th of 2006 I was placed in a kind of void. I had been "keeping on keeping on" at the survival level for years, without much Joy other than the Joy I felt around Tara Singh. With due respect to my former wife, we were no longer on the same page. There was a division of basic life purpose which separated us. I yearned to simplify and be with the Spirit. She seemed to want a better kitchen. This division became too great after a year-and-a-half without Taraji. It reached its critical mass in the fall of 2007, and I moved out to live in the house next to our art studio.

We were definitely in transition now. I had made a stand and faced my fears. I did not know where I was going, but I knew I could not go on the way it had been. I was "at the branching in the road."

> *When you come to the place where the branch in the road is quite apparent, you cannot go ahead. You must go either one way or the other. For now if you go straight ahead, the way you went before you reached the branch, you will go nowhere. The whole purpose of coming this far was to decide which branch you will take now. The way you came no longer matters. It can no longer serve. No one who reaches this far can make the wrong decision, although he can delay. And there is no part of the journey that seems more hopeless and futile than standing where the road branches, and not deciding on which way to go. (ACIM; Text; Chapter 22, Section IV, The Branching in the Road)*

Well, The Christ had other plans for me. It was like a vortex of circumstances that took over my life. I got a flyer in the mail that one of my earlier teachers, Sondra Ray, who had introduced me to *A Course in Miracles* in 1985 at a Loving Relationships Training in Philadelphia, was coming to town to do a workshop on Prosperity. I definitely needed that. So I sent in my registration and showed up in the downtown Philadelphia Sheraton Hotel. I had not seen Sondra Ray in 20 years. It was like a blast from the past.

This was the miracle I needed. We reconnected on a very deep soul level, as we had very similar spiritual interests. We had these things in common: she was a student of *A Course in Miracles* like myself; she had practiced Ho'oponopono for years, a deep forgiveness process from Hawaii (in fact, she introduced me to that as well); she was a lover of India and still took a group every year to Babaji's ashram; she was a published writer and could appreciate my writings, though none of mine were published yet.

In less than two months of being in this vortex of Sondra Ray's energy, I knew for certain I was to be with her. I signed up for the India Quest 2008. I accompanied Sondra to workshops in Asheville, NC and Nashville, TN. We rose in Love in Nashville, and I asked for her hand in marriage, even though the legal arrangements for my divorce were not yet fully in place. I completed them before March when I was to travel to Los Angeles where Sondra lived in Marina Del Rey, then from there to accompany her to Greece and India.

I went through a barrage of disapproval and attack from my friends and ex-wife, but I knew I had to just face down my fear and guilt (very related to fear), and just keep moving. I stepped out of fear in the spring of 2008 when I left Philadelphia for good, to embrace my new destiny with Sondra Ray, with two suitcases in my hands. I left everything material to my former wife which I had accumulated over 30 years. Two properties, two cars, and everything else. And I never looked back. I "placed the future," truly, "in the "Hands of God."

15. Embracing Love

Love dawns in the heart ready to receive it. Tara Singh had awakened in me a Love beyond words, beyond the confines of usual emotions, outside of the parameters of thought itself. He had brought my mind to stillness and silence unprecedented. Only once before, with a sage I met in India with Sondra Ray in 1987, could I say what this stillness and silence felt like. But with Tara Singh, this state of Divine emptiness was sustained over a long period of time. My association with him over seventeen years gave me plenty of opportunities to experience in his presence the un-experienceable—to make contact with *moments outside of time*, as he called them.

I need not go into these encounters I had with him here. They are well discussed in my book, *Miracles with My Master, Tara Singh* (bit.ly/TSRay). But I feel I do need to mention that a Teacher is very much needed to take us to these dimensions beyond the conditioning of our *normal* thought processes. A teacher will see things in us we do not see—self-imposed limitations and insecurities we may or may not be seeing or admitting. One of the most compassionate things they do for us is to point them out. And this "undoing" process is their principal role. The function of the Holy Spirit working through them is to help us correct ourselves. Therefore, the Teacher imparts in us a *love for correction*—without the tinge of guilt. It is a Holy Relationship of the highest order. To have a real Master Teacher is one of the greatest blessings of Life.

There is a version of "love" the ego makes up, and the *Course* calls this "specialness." It either says, "I am not complete, and you have what I need to complete me, so I am going to love you so I can 'get' what you have to make me whole." It calls this the *special love relationship*. Then there is the version where, "I do not feel whole, and I need you as a scapegoat of all my problems, so I have you around to blame for all of my shortcomings." The *Course* calls this the *special hate relationship*. Neither is real Love, but many couples fall into the unconscious trap of these main forms of special relationships. These also can be acted out in the workplace. Most areas of our life are susceptible to falling "victim" of special relationships. It is the way of the world.

What does it mean to embrace Love? What are the attributes of true Love? How do we awaken it, discover it, have it certainly in our life? It is the whole purpose of incarnating, this awakening. How can we get our priorities straight, and step out of the momentum of narcissism that has swept over the Western cultures—our culture?

Love, which created me, is what I am.
(ACIM; Workbook; Lesson #229)

When the cards are on the table, and we are told the truth by a Being Who is the incarnation of Truth, we see that our Self-Identity is Love Itself. It is not a "woo-woo new age concept," but rather a basic tenet of Life. It is not something we ever have to "seek" with the notion we do not have it already. Love has its attributes, and it is also aware of those conditions of which it is not—anger, fear, jealousy, attachment, grievances, resentment, insecurity, vengeance, pride, low self-esteem, dependence, entrapment, etc. One could list a compendium of qualities *unlike Love.* But what would be the attributes that come with Love? What is our real function here on earth, to realize the Absolute Love within us?

> ***I have a function God would have me fill.***
>
> *It is your Father's holy Will that you complete Himself, and that your Self shall be His sacred Son, forever pure as He, of love created and in love preserved, extending love, creating in its name, forever one with God and with your Self.*
>
> *(ACIM; Workbook; Lesson #192)*

Listen to the loftiness of these words: "Your Self shall be His sacred Son, forever pure as He, of love created and in love preserved, extending love, creating in its name, forever one with God and with your Self."

How could we ever be unclear why we are here in this life with a direction this elevated and holy? The result of fulfilling our function here is Pure Joy. Are we willing to go for this function? I know everybody has something "other" that they are doing—working in an office, in a store, on a construction site etc.—but can we see in whatever we are doing we can bring our holy function to it? The very people we see in our life every day, we can begin to extend Love to them.

Can we open ourselves to receive this Self-Identity into our awareness? This Oneness is already there in us. Why can we not seem to fully embrace it? This realization and feeling should be the cause for elation! What is preventing us from the Pure Joy that Love holds out as its extension? Could it be that we believe we have other functions for ourselves we have imposed on our lives? And these other functions gain so much priority and momentum that we forget the one main function our Creator gave to us. So one of the blocks to feeling the Love of God is that we are unwilling to let go of all the other functions we made up.

The purpose of my life is to embrace my Self Identity, which is Love. "Love is all there is," as the Beatles said in the song, "All you need is Love." An oversimplification perhaps, but the truth is spoken. *A Course in Miracles* takes this to a higher level in its teachings, in making clear the door to this Love. It says, "Forgiveness represents your function here." Forgiveness is the doorway to Love's realization in this dimension. It is our function.

Forgiveness is my function as the light of the world.
(ACIM; Workbook; Lesson #62)

The light of Love will not dawn on the planet, or in us, without the function of complete forgiveness being fulfilled in us. This is our main job, so to speak, in taking a body here. We are to embrace Love through forgiveness—we are to awaken to our true Self of Love, through the means of complete and unequivocal forgiveness.

What would that be? What is the forgiveness the *Course* lays out as my function? It is an important question because, like Love, the ego has its false version of forgiveness as well. And we have to distinguish between the two.

- The ego's version of forgiveness: You did something to me, or you did something offensive or wrong, and because I am so good and righteous, I will "let you off the hook." You don't deserve it, you are a real "sinner," but I will sacrifice myself in denying this "truth of your badness," and just overlook your inequities. I will "love" you even though you are despicable in your actions.

- The Holy Spirit's version of forgiveness has a different focus on self-responsibility. In this version I see that I was also connected to the vibrational match of the problem arising around the wrong committed; if a mistake was made, or a relationship failed, I am responsible for that in my world. I need not feel guilty. I was using my ego's thought system in which to gain some kind of specialness. So I am just as much a part of the problem as the "other."

- It is my responsibility to admit my error and to seek Divine transmutation of my errors through real forgiveness. No one is guilty in this ego's play, because I can step outside of my ego and connect with my True Self, in which the infraction never occurred. I was operating as my false self, my ego self, projecting a world of problems, issues, dualities, and dynamics of specialness. From my memory bank of traumas and problems, I just repeated a similar scenario of the past onto the present. My fear of the future is just my unwillingness to let my ego go and arrive fully in the present as my true Self—Love.

- But I can decide to use my God Created Self in which all parties are absolved. No one is guilty within this Self. The whole complex of the ego's world is rendered meaningless, and therefore worthy of letting completely go. I release it as it releases me. All people benefit from this internal shift of paradigms.

We do not have to wait to embrace this total forgiveness. It does not take time. But our tendencies of unwillingness still want to blame another or ourselves for our shortcomings and problems. Remember the "responsibility for sight" spoken about above. We ask for everything that seems to happen to us because we needed to forgive it and let it go. Once we see we are the "cause" of our pains and sufferings, we can join the crusade of true forgiveness to undo these ego "causes" and embrace the only real Cause that makes any sense: "Love, which created me, is what I am," is Lesson #229. We are the "Effect" of Love when we have mastered total and complete forgiveness. "I am forever an Effect of God." is Lesson # 326. Love only creates Love; therefore, I am an effect in the Mind of Love, of God.

When I reconnected with Sondra Ray in December of 2007 I was open to receive a new life. Embracing Love came along with embracing the Unknown. I knew I could not go backward. I knew I had a function "God would have me fill," although I did not know exactly what that was to look like. I knew the dynamism of Sondra Ray was drawing me forward into a new life, and the Divine Mother played a role in this call to a totally different purpose. I was entering a domain of freedom I had known before. I was going into the future by facing my highest aspirations (and worst fears) right in the present. And Life was cooperating in leaps and bounds.

I was not so concerned with any of my "stuff." To be free of it all was making me more and more certain of this turn of events—in my acceptance of my destiny. I left Philadelphia more or less penniless, but it did not matter. I knew that the joy of life with Sondra Ray would far surpass any accumulation of material wealth I had managed up until that time in my life. I felt so free to call the divorce lawyer and say, on the day I was leaving my "old life" to go to California, "Give her everything!" He was a bit shocked. I guess people don't do that much. They "fight it out" for years or decide on percentages. I was more or less sidestepping the whole issue by relinquishing everything. I felt so free when I got on that plane. I was embracing Love in a way I had never done before—and it was of a Joy beyond the most elated bodies of former experience. I cannot describe it in mere words.

My biggest concern was a vehicle I had just purchased. I would not be able to take it with me, and I still "owed" a considerable amount on the loan. I called up the dealer and asked them to repossess it. This is something I never would have done in my old life of conformity. That would have been a shameful thing to do. No one in my family ever defaulted on a loan. Well, I felt some humiliation about this. After all was said and done, and they repossessed the vehicle, I still owed ten thousand dollars on it. I paid it off for two years. So even that was not insurmountable, and Life provided for the restoration of my financial order.

Embracing Love does not always come without challenges. This is the point I am making here. What the ego may see as a "sacrifice" or a "loss" could be the very Action of Life working to move us up the ascension ladder of our evolution. I could even make the point it was more compassionate to leave my old marriage (long after it had ceased to have a life of matrimonial bliss) than to stay in it based on family pressures or social judgments. We both had tried to come to a higher place in it, and I had to face it was over. I was in a new embrace of the Unknown. And I felt the blessing of Life upon this new direction.

Could I have felt "guilty" for leaving my companion of thirty years? Yes. Was she perceiving herself with the emotional short end of the deal? Yes. Did she feel abandoned without me around as the main breadwinner? Yes. Did I trust that this move was better for both of us? Yes. Was I embracing Love even though my ex-partner was perceiving me as the "devil." Yes. In most transitions in our life, there are all kinds of unknown factors at play. One cannot control the feelings of others, but we do have dominion over our own. What was feeling like a log-jam, or a dead-end in my life, was finally over and opened up. I could take a breath of fresh air, even though there were parts of this transition that seemed to make my life more difficult. In truth, they made my life more open and free. Embracing Love will always bring a person more freedom. And I could forgive myself for whatever this new embrace looked like for myself and all involved, including my former partner of thirty years.

Embracing Love. We all say we want to do that. We all say love and happiness go together. But we all experience suffering, with the adage that "love bears all." But what Love bears was not made by Love—rather, it was made by the thoughts of the ego which have been separated, for whatever reason, from the Source of Love. Embracing Love is no less than declaring all that is not pure Joy has no place in our life. We bear the suffering until we undo the causes in ourselves which make it up in the first place. The Love of correction is what we need in the face of suffering, not the belief that we have to "bear it." It is not the Will of a benign Creator that we ever suffer. Painful situations, relationships, events, and conditions have their roots in a mind that is vibrating in lower levels of feeling: insecurity, anger, fear, shame, loneliness, jealousy, greed, etc. Embracing Love is to rise above these feelings, to "step out" of these *causes* for suffering. Forgiveness is the means, and a palpable and direct contact with the Christ within us is the necessity.

> ***If it helps you, think of me holding your hand and leading you. And I assure you this will be no idle fantasy.*** *(ACIM; Workbook; Lesson #70)*

With this help, we can step out of the ego-self we made and embrace the Love we are—free of all suffering.

PART 4

Creating Heaven on Earth

16.
Christ in Ourselves

When we look inside what do we see? Grief? Pain? Suffering? Regret? A general malaise of remorse over a doleful past, or a painful present, or an uncertain future? Or do we see ourselves on top of the world? We played our cards in Life very well and Life has been a blessing. Or, do we see peak experiences of unusual happiness—a short vacation from all of the drudgery of routine, but then “back to the grind on Monday?” Do we see ourselves as basically good people, mostly content with our life, but having a slight nagging feeling of “is this all there is?” Perhaps we are in a bad situation that will take some time to play out, with consequences from past actions for which we are now paying off the debt. Many external conditions come into play when we look within and ask ourselves, “What do I see?”

We often say in our seminars on relationships when we talk about Spiritual Masters in our life—“Until we are walking on water, healing the blind and raising the dead, we have something to clear.” We set our standards high, merely because we think the proper use of this Life is to rise and evolve as high as we possibly can Spiritually—which encompasses all areas of our life and being. Spiritual intimacy, for instance, applies to having intimacy in all our relationships in all areas of Life.

This "looking within" is twofold. One, it entails the status quo of where we are right now—with all of the conditions in which we find ourselves: with mate, family, colleagues and friends, work and how we spend our productive life, and how we spend our leisure life. Two, it also entails our aspirations and dreams. To whom do we look up? We *Look Within* to *Look Up, Above and Beyond*. Reaching for the stars from earth implies we have a Divine Purpose here that is higher than just our personality traits, our professional goals, our survival mechanisms, and our people skills.

What is our status quo? Where are we right now in our life? What defines our satisfaction? What do we need to let go of; and what do we need to strengthen and give more from our deepest desire? We could even make a couple of lists:

The things in my life I would like to release:

1. ____________
2. ____________
3. ____________
4. ____________
5. __________etc.

The things in my life I would like to strengthen:

1. ____________
2. ____________
3. ____________
4. ____________
5. __________etc.

And then an affirmation we use to draw to us what we would like to see manifest in our life:

I am so happy and grateful I now have

1. ___________
2. ___________
3. ___________
4. ___________
5. _________etc.

Notice how you feel when you say this, especially about the things you would like to manifest that have not shown up yet!

Getting into the vibration of the feeling around that manifestation is a good approach. It creates an energy of trust and faith that the Life Force wants us to have everything that enhances our purpose here. Focusing on the "appearance" of "not having" (whatever it is) keeps us in the results of not having. This is a sense of lack. Because thoughts and feelings always precede their results, immersing ourselves in the Joy of having is far more attractive than dwelling on the status quo of not having—and a sense of lack. Our attention could be on a relationship, a family member, an attitude, a position of work, an investment, a project that is inspiring us onward. This forward movement into the feelings of having is very essential. The Joy of an abundant flow is more attractive than the doldrums of a stagnant sense of lack. For those of us who have listened to Esther Hicks, this is the classic "Law of Attraction" which she so well describes and practices. And it is consistent with the laws discussed in *A Course in Miracles.*

> *Few appreciate the real power of the mind, and no one remains fully aware of it all the time. However, if you hope to spare yourself from fear there are some things you must realize, and realize fully. The mind is very powerful, and never loses its creative force. It never sleeps. Every instant it is creating. It is hard to recognize that thought and belief combine into a power surge that can literally move mountains. It appears at first glance that to believe such power about yourself is arrogant, but that is not the real reason you do not believe it. You prefer to believe that*

> *your thoughts cannot exert real influence because you are actually afraid of them. This may allay awareness of the guilt, but at the cost of perceiving the mind as impotent. If you believe that what you think is ineffectual you may cease to be afraid of it, but you are hardly likely to respect it. There are no idle thoughts. All thinking produces form at some level.*
>
> *(ACIM; Text; Chapter 2; Section VI; ¶ 9)*

"There are no idle thoughts. All thinking produces form at some level." The acceptance that our thought always produces form makes the choice between joy or sorrow our responsibility. The thoughts that spearhead feelings are our domain because we are in charge of our minds.

I rule my mind, which I alone must rule.
(ACIM; Workbook; Lesson #236)

The Christ in ourselves is up to us to see. This awareness has to do with the quality of our mind which we use to navigate in this world. Our mind is our domain, and we have it to use according to our free will. Christ is in our mind, but somehow we don't give attention to access Him. He is fully Present, but somehow we are absent, or only partially attentive to making a contact with Him. What thoughts are we thinking; what feelings are we maintaining? These are the determiners of the contact we make with the Christ in us.

Thoughts have power. Thoughts of Love and expansion are miracles that undo other thoughts of fear and limitation. Every Lesson in *A Course in Miracles* is a miracle. Every Lesson is a "thought of the Christ" in our mind. We do not need to wonder while studying the *Course*, "When are miracles going to show up?" The Workbook gives us 365 Miracles, one a day for a year. They are potent, and do not have a "shelf life." We can pick them up any time to lift us into another realm of sacred reality. They unravel and undo the misperceptions we have made. Thoughts and feelings not supremely joyous are the only real problems to undo. Unfortunately, we have elevated these thoughts to the status of *reality*.

Have we not suffered enough to accept the help? Are we clear on the fact that *cause and effect* is a matter of the mind, and which thoughts we maintain in that mind? It is best to bring the mind to silence, to empty, to prepare an open vessel to receive the Thoughts of God. The Thoughts of God are those of the Christ in us—and to access them we have to clear out the ego's thought system of fear, control, domination, manipulation, etc. "How does one do that?" people ask. There is not a "how" to it. Rather, it is an awareness of the perennial limitations of our very thought system, and a willingness to let go of it. In this empty space of silence and stillness the Holy Spirit fills us with the light of God, with the thoughts and feelings of God, which would always result in Peace and Joy.

There is a dynamic in this realization. It is a relinquishment, then an emptiness, then a capacity to receive, in that order. What is it we are relinquishing? Our "need to know." What is this emptiness? This is our realization we do not know and don't need to, because the Christ in us *knows*. What is the capacity to receive? That is a trust that Divine Forces of Life will send down the right and perfect people, situation, opportunity, insight for us to thrive and fulfill our complete destiny in this life. The Christ in ourselves helps us come to an awareness of our true Self, in actuality. In that awareness, there is nothing to do, no "how" to learn, and no set of rules which keep us bound to our ego. All notions of a "self" that falls short of our greatest potential are left behind. The interstellar possibilities abound and emerge in our life. Something new is born in us.

The holy Christ is born in me today.

Watch with me, angels, watch with me today. Let all God's holy Thoughts surround me, and be still with me while Heaven's Son is born. Let earthly sounds be quiet, and the sights to which I am accustomed disappear. Let Christ be welcomed where He is at home. And let Him hear the sounds He understands, and see but sights that show His Father's Love. Let Him no longer be a stranger here, for He is born again in me today.

(ACIM; Workbook; Lesson #303)

The Second Coming is the birth of the Christ in us. When He is seen no more as an abstract figure from history who died for our sins and resurrected from death to save us, He will dawn in our minds—in all his sisters and brothers who yearn to know the truth, the absolute and Immortality of Life itself. We will realize He comes again in this very moment, as the Christ in Ourselves.

Watch with me, angels, watch with me today. Let all God's holy Thoughts surround me, and be still with me while Heaven's Son is born.

17. Christ in Our Family

Family is the beginning of our existence here. It is the home of most of our karmic patterns to work out in this lifetime. This "working out" implies some conditions need to be transcended or moved through, or some corrections need to be made to liberate our souls to their highest ascension. Freedom within and without the family mindset is absolutely necessary. Most of us have had some past to outgrow and to release concerning our family, relatives, and ancestors. Ultimately, we desire to be forgiven and released from the family mind; and they, in turn, desire the same freedom. The world of the family mind is very intense; most of our conditioning begins there and holds influence over our beliefs and behaviors.

Without sounding like a family criticism, it took me a lot of soul-searching and inner work on myself to rise above the limitations of my family's mind. Mind you, there were great things that I learned from parents, grandparents, aunts and uncles, sibling and cousins—and stories about ancestors—and I can trace my artistic ability through my mother's side of the family, and my incessant desire to question things from my father's side of the family. At the same time, I wanted the independent lifestyle of an artist that did not conform to the more conventional choices that my parents would have wanted for me. I went to the Cleveland Institute of Art to study painting, drawing, and sculpture—basically the fine arts. And there was not much in the practical "get a job after college" department of this kind of education. It was broad and deep education in pondering Beauty—and pushing the boundaries of self-expression—but it was not so translatable into a fixed position in the marketplace.

My Uncle Harold was an electrical engineer. My grandfather was a self-employed small businessman. My father worked as an operator of our town's local water treatment plant. These were the men in my life. They were good men. My mother was from a family of seven children and had her college degree in business administration, at a time when women did not go to college quite so much. She helped my grandparents with their small business. We lived in Mount Vernon, a small town in Ohio, amidst the rolling hills and farmland of Knox County, toward the middle of that state. It was a semi pastoral life. Though we lived in the town, there was a sense of nature's peace and quiet that surrounded our environment.

My mom and grandmother were determined that we had a proper respect for God, and they were members of the Gay Street United Methodist Church. So my sister and I were taken to Sunday School most weekends. One could say there was a presence of Christ in our family, but it was mostly on Sundays and holidays. The rest of the week was focused on work or school or just plain survival. I remember we would say the grace at meals, but that would not be so much of an authentic spiritual connection for me as it was just the repetition of a family ritual. I am not sure anyone was in touch with the deeper vibrations of a constant inner Joy that would go along with true grace. But, we did the best we could at the time with what we had. God's Providence was present, though not so fully noticed on a moment-to-moment basis.

A family is a set of relationships: Father, Mother, Child or multiple Children. I came from a traditional family. My parents were "married for life" through thick and thin, and that never changed. I had one sister. My parents were not always super happy together, but they were civilized. Their generation just stuck it out, regardless of emotional ups and downs. Our family life was geared mostly toward work and school. We lived near my grandparents, so they influenced my upbringing. They were happy people, for the most part. They loved life, from what I could tell.

When I moved out at eighteen to go to art school, I felt like I was stepping out of conventions. In many ways I was, but the values of coming from a very conventional family were still in me, and art school was a cultural shock. Coupled with the fact that the Cleveland Institute of Art was in an urban environment, and a ghetto at that, I felt completely out of my element. Christ in that environment seemed to have very little relevance to the place, to the situation, and to those people with whom I associated—fellow students and professors alike. I was immediately outside the realm of the family, and this was more of an eye-opener than I was willing to admit. I felt isolated. Those were difficult years. But I more or less stuffed it and postponed any inklings of a spiritual life that were more related to my traditional religious upbringing. Not only did my parents not understand why I was going to art school, but I also am not so sure I understood it either. All I knew at the time was I did not want, at least from an intellectual standpoint, a conventional life.

I met another artist, Susan Sipos, in 1978 and we got married after spending the summer traveling together in Europe. We were betrothed in the Catholic church in Cleveland, Ohio because her father was Catholic. And I liked the architecture in the church. It seemed that despite four years of art school some of the same conventional values were still ingrained in me, which I could not shake off despite a very unconventional education. Susan and I moved to Philadelphia in 1980 for me to go to graduate school in art at Temple University. So after another two years of academia, I received my Master's Degree in Fine Arts. Yet, I was sick of academia by then, so pursuing a life in that world of college professorship was not for me. And that was how "artists" made a living—professing art. I had a notion I would just be a painter, an artist in my studio, and something miraculous would happen in that department of my life. It was a naïve notion. I did not have the gregarious personality to promote myself in the ways more successful artists have done to succeed in the past, present and future. I was a bit of a loner. I had a bit of a chip on my shoulder. I was a bit frightened and angry about the whole matter. I did manage to have a drawing purchased by the Philadelphia Museum of Art out of a show I won first prize.

By 1984 I was doing Yoga, and then Rebirthing. Although art always had a spiritual side to it for me, Yoga and Breathwork were modalities designed to get a person in touch with his or her Divine Nature. I began to embrace a spiritual life in tandem with my life as an artist. I met up with *A Course in Miracles* around 1985; and it was like the Christ coming back into my life in a meaningful way, without having to revert to the Church approach to spirituality. My family accepted the fact I did things my way, but we did not have a means for common ground. They accepted I was not conventional but did not understand it. I think they knew I needed to paint and draw but could not see the need for that themselves in day-to-day life. I was disenthralled from my family, perhaps even detached, and the presence of Christ in our family at that point seemed distant, dormant, and perhaps even on sabbatical.

Then I met Tara Singh in 1989 as mentioned above, and he became my Teacher. He was giving a workshop in Stony

Point, New York over the Easter weekend. When I met him face to face, it was *like the Christ* entered my life in the flesh and turned my world upside down. *A Course in Miracles* was the vehicle for this relationship, but it was a Life for Life encounter in which someone of greater wisdom and spiritual contact served to bring me into that higher place within myself. This relationship continued for seventeen years until Tara Singh's passing in 2006. Not a day has gone by since then that I do not think of him, and the hand of the Master on my shoulder.

What we discover soon when studying with a Spiritual Master is that we are tremendously conditioned. Our families, our society, our educational and religious systems, our experiences all form a conglomerate of the personality which by and large shapes our fate, our relationships, and our situations and actions in Life. And this conditioning limits us. Christ is amidst all of this "family" conditioning, yet we are so determined to "make ourselves up," as we go, we seldom stop to question this ego-self with whom we identify. It seems our sense of self goes along with an accumulation of experiences in many areas of our life, and the family being one of the major influencers of our conditioning. Even in rebellion, these conditions still form and shape us, determining our direction and destiny. We are as if trapped in the self we made.

This conditioning of the mind is the first thing a real Teacher will begin to question and "undo", and we will feel stripped away; out of our comfort zone; turned upside down by his questions. This kind of an "undoing" or "dismantling" of the self was not something I quite signed up for, but I knew it was necessary for my spiritual evolution. Tara Singh was a Master of "undoing." He questioned everything of thought itself and brought his students to "the stillness of the peace of God," which our thought could not put together. He could bring our thought to silence. One was held accountable for everything internally going on in their life. He did not care if one had a string of college degrees. He was concerned with the quality of the inner person—how pure was he to live a life of fearlessness and service amidst those around him.

My family did not understand Tara Singh and my relationship with him, any more than they understood why I would want to devote a greater portion of my life to painting and drawing pictures. Nevertheless, when the light of a greater reason kindles a flame in the heart of one's own inner truth, he cannot run away or deny the grace that has been bestowed upon him. He becomes a servant of that light, and the person responsible for that transmission of light is the Teacher—deserving of a deep reverence beyond anything else we may ever know in this life. Far greater than even respect for one's own blood parents. The Family of the Spirit is known from the remarkable clarity and Love of the Christ. And when He walked into my life in the form of Tara Singh, I was transformed forever.

18.
Christ in Our Work Place

The Maha Avatar Sri Sri 1008 Herakhan Babaji said, "Work is worship; idleness is death." He put forth the premise that Self-Realization is immersed in what He called Karma Yoga—work dedicated to service in some way, to better yourself, your family, and your society and the people around you. The Christ is no different in His directions that we fulfill ourselves here in these dimensions of earthly existence.

I have a function God would have me fill.
(ACIM; Workbook; Lesson #192

What is that for you? What gives you deep satisfaction? There could be an aspiration to your work, even if it appears to be a mundane task. Like I said, I graduated from Art School, twice, without much direction of what work I would do to earn my bread. Painting was the work I loved. It was not the work I did to earn my bread at first. That came much later.

I had a very thorough education in the crafts in Cleveland—so this made me very good with my hands. I could put anything together. So it did not require much on the part of educating myself to apply that sense of craft to the building trades. I was a good carpenter; tile setter, electrician, and I could even do my own plumbing when I chose to. I put these skills to work and earned my bread, so to speak, while I maintained my passion for painting and drawing. I had a studio, a house, and a second house we rented out to finance the studio. My wife then was a ceramic artist, so she made pottery in the back half of the studio. She also liked plants, so horticultural jobs were part of the bailiwick of our multi-tasking professions.

When I met Tara Singh I had already been to India a couple of times. I had been a Sikh who wore a turban for three years while studying Yoga with Yogi Bhajan. I had been doing rebirthing for 5 years, and reading *A Course in Miracles* for about the same amount of time. I had a small kitchen and bathroom construction business, specializing in fine art tile and marble installations. I had a rhythm in my studio of painting. I was living a life that seemed to be "independent of the herd." And, there were a few men who helped me in my work, but they were part-time, on-demand. I had no "employees." Uncle Lenny, my Italian neighbor across the street, would help me sometimes—but he was not a craftsman, so I had to constantly run quality control over his work. Often it was more trouble than it was worth. But, I loved Uncle Lenny just the same. We would sit in his kitchen and listen to the radio with Rush Limbaugh, even though I was more or less a liberal at the time. Even that did not bother me. I loved Uncle Lenny.

You could not have called me a "businessman." Though, with my clients, I exercised an impeccability of craft and contractual agreements that made them love my work. So there always was work to do—but most of the time I did this alone. I would hire a plumber, Norman Schmidt, when I needed one. He was of German descent. He was absolutely incorrigible—but he always got the job done in half the time another plumber would, for half the price. And it always worked. It got covered up anyway, so over fastidiousness was not necessary for plumbing. And his work never leaked. I loved Norman. He would insult me and call me names, and I would love him even more. Sometimes I would hire a tile setter if I had a big job, and sometimes a carpenter's assistant. But more often than not I found another person would just get in the way. I was not so good at delegating. My hand had to be on the material—on the final product. The clients knew this, appreciated this, and wanted an "artist" doing their work. So I functioned in this capacity as a master craftsman for hire. Eventually, I would do the design as well on the kitchens and bathrooms. I liked it, as I like "putting things together."

But one time Tara Singh came to Philadelphia to check in on a service project some of us were doing in North Philadelphia. Along with a fellow *ACIM* student, Alexander Barnes, we had a soup kitchen and a halfway house for addicts to get clean. I had helped build some shower rooms for homeless people to have a daily shower, and I was taking Tara Singh over to see these projects. While driving in the car through the ghetto he asked me, "Why are you still at the survival level?" I was shocked. Even with all this "do-gooder" activity I had given to these service projects, he was spot-on right. I was still functioning at the "survival level" of physical and personal struggles and preoccupations. The fears of survival still possessed my consciousness.

We arrived at the *Miracle House* and met Alexander there. Climbing up the dark and narrow stairwell to the second floor, I did not know what had quite hit me. The drug addicts who were living in the house getting clean were very welcoming of Tara Singh. They were like little children. Uneducated. Rather crude in demeanor, yet, they had a kind of simple reverence that exceeded their downtrodden existence. They listened attentively when Tara Singh talked to them about finding something they liked to do—and doing it. In other words, "be productive." And that amounted to the same thing Babaji told us: "Work is worship; idleness is death." The meeting went on for about thirty minutes. Then we toured the rest of the building and finally got back in the car, driving through the ghetto on our return to my house in Manayunk. I was still in shock. All my notions of "doing good" were but a smokescreen to hide the facts of my conditioned life—at the "level of survival."

There is no "special work." Action is action, and it's either under the Holy Spirit's guidance or the ego's guidance. There is not a partial place in the middle for a mixture of the two. "You need to transcend the 'survival level,' and to do this you need miracles!" This is what Tara Singh told me on the trip back home. I was seeking some kind of work that was "special" in my charitable service. And then in my other work I was serving my clients, mostly according to terms to please them, making them "special." And in my Artwork I was again making that "special" and thinking it was more lofty than building a shower in a bathroom, let's say. And there were aspects of all the work that I felt was a drudgery. So back then I did not have the notion that "Work is worship," or that I was entitled to miracles in the context of my actions.

Gradually I began to transform the quality of my attention to consider all my actions sacred. Even if it was mixing cement, sawing a board, painting a picture, writing up a detailed project proposal, drawing the likeness of a face, or working in a soup kitchen for the poor—all actions were turned over to the guidance of the Holy Spirit to sanctify my work. Christ in my work place was a different approach. And it was a decision to be guided, and not assume that *I knew* what to do.

The outlook starts with this:

Today I will make no decisions by myself.

This means that you are choosing not to be the judge of what to do. But it must also mean you will not judge the situations where you will be called upon to make response. For if you judge them, you have set the rules for how you should react to them. And then another answer cannot but produce confusion and uncertainty and fear. (ACIM; Text; Chapter 30; Section I; The Rules for Decision)

Even in my common actions of working as a contractor, I was choosing not to make decisions "by myself." But rather, ask first what to do. This establishes a direct relationship with the Holy Spirit whose Will for us is perfect happiness. The beautiful part of working with this force of clear direction is when we find ourselves moving away from having a happy day, we can "right our course" by admitting, "I must have been wrong." I was trying to make a decision "by myself," and this threw me into dissatisfaction, discontent, or some negative emotion that was not Pure Joy. It's time to "reboot" in this situation, which is disengaging from the scene long enough to get a new perspective. A new course of action will be given, and this is directly from the Holy Spirit that speaks to anyone willing to listen—in this mental state of emptiness. There is no guilt or failure in asking for help from the Holy Spirit to give us a "happy day." That is His function—to lead us. "I will step back and let Him lead the way." Now, this Lesson #155 makes sense.

We all find ourselves in a situation. We may not always feel the Light of the Peace of God. We may not always feel that the Grace of Life is upon us. We may be in a mild doldrum or a pit of despair; loved ones may pass away; work could go awry; our actions may fall short of giving us a sense of fulfillment. In these moments we need the Holy Spirit the most. Christ in the workplace is this very invocation for guidance to make our actions count—only to lead us ever closer to the perfect happiness and fulfillment God has created for us to be. We are not bereft of hope or happiness anytime.

The "work of the day" is always Love. The Christ is in us to master it and this is the workplace of our life. It is not special to a job, or a project we are doing, or a particular set of parameters that we are endeavoring to bring our excellence to bear. Every instant is a moment in His timelessness.

> *To love is good, too: love being difficult. For one human being to love another: that is perhaps the most difficult of all our tasks, the ultimate, the last test and proof, the work for which all other work is but preparation.*
>
> *There is scarcely anything more difficult than to love one another. That it is work, day labor, day labor, God knows there is no other word for it.*
>
> ***— Rainer Maria Rilke***

Our "single purpose" is to receive the Love and the Grace from a Power beyond ourselves, and to extend that Love. We expect so much from the ones around us. Can we let them go to be themselves? And can we find the Peace and Joy already within us, unconditional, present without reasons that we would make? No one person can give us this Love. We awaken it in ourselves, as it is already there. This is what we carry as our true Identity placed in the spark of our Being from time immemorial. This is what we have to give, and this is the Love of work that the Masters would have us perform. This is the Christ in our workplace. This is the "work of the day."

Work is Worship. Idleness is death. — Sri Babaji

19. Christ in Our Community

We are joined to live in a community of infinite atoms and molecules, in a cosmos of infinite possibilities. We are in communities of families, friends, professions, teams and towns, churches, organizations, social mediums, and collections of individuals gathered together for the common good of all. The domains of our communities are legion. What happens to one in those domains happens and affects all others. This is a Law not only of the natural universe but it is also the Law of Love.

> ***Today I learn the law of love; that what I give my brother is my gift to me.***
>
> *This is Your law, my Father, not my own. I have not understood what giving means and thought to save what I desired for myself alone. And as I looked upon the treasure that I thought I had, I found an empty place where nothing ever was or is or will be.*

Who can share a dream? And what can an illusion offer me? Yet he whom I forgive will give me gifts beyond the worth of anything on earth. Let my forgiven brothers fill my store with Heaven's treasures, which alone are real. Thus is the law of love fulfilled. And thus Your Son arises and returns to You.

How near we are to one another, as we go to God. How near is He to us. How close the ending of the dream of sin, and the redemption of the Son of God.

(ACIM; Workbook; Lesson # 344)

The community of people who form our world is the treasure of a gift so vast we can hardly fathom their importance in the total scheme of our life. We have a destiny to know Love in the absolute sense, which formed the stars and is the Cause for all our real desires. The Law of Love asks only one question to us—"What do you have to give?"

The Light came across the Universe into our souls to sustain us and keep us safe from all harm. We have been engulfed by a Love so great we can hardly appreciate its vastness. Even one breath is a glorious gift of Being that rivals the most massive movements of storms that blow across an atmosphere enveloping our whole planet. God's inhale and exhale breathe whole solar systems of Beauty into existence in the blink of an eye. And yet, we have dominion over this all-pervasive outpouring of Beauty. It belongs to us to give. Where in this picture is there room for isolation or doubt? Where is there cause for withholding our love, meting it out to some and stingily keeping it away from others?

"What I give my brother, is my gift to me." What am I giving my brother, then? That would have to be what I am also giving myself. Giving is the key to anything real in our action of Community. The commune of human existence is interdependent in myriads of ways. There is no one way to give, except that it be from the Source of Love so all-inclusive that there is no tinge of separation we ever feel from the whole of creation. We cannot take one breath except by the Grace of God Who created us. And the realization of this is a reason for a Joy that rises above reason and goes far beyond the most elated bodies of physical existence and experience. Contact with that Source is what we extend in all of our actions of giving. Then the "thing" we give does not matter. One flower given in this garland of sacred delight is worth a million dollars of philanthropy. The contact with the Source is made, and this is what we give to our Communities. It is our "day labor" to do this, as Rilke said. It is like a Communion of the Holy Christ in us and our Communities.

Connection begins with one simple act. Mother Teresa said one simple act of giving that you put your whole heart into and complete with great Love is worth more than whole projects to instigate social change. She once said passionately about the work she did for the poor, "This is not social work!" It was the Work of the Christ to take action in an unbroken chain of small acts of giving to the people in need in her community—with every act done with great Love. This is what we need to do everywhere—in the communities of our families, of our jobs, of our social media, of our circles of friends, of our clients, students or customers we serve. Each person in this Community represents the whole; each action we do for our brother or sister is an action we take to support the whole. "Small is beautiful," said the economist E.F. Schumacher. Rather than be concerned with the "bigger is better" mentality, think in terms of one single act of Love followed by another single act of Love. And this way a chain is formed in the endless Chain of Divine Love that holds the Community together.

What we do to further our work in the Community is our ministry. Our ministries are our email contacts, our mailing lists, our Facebook friends, our Twitter and Instagram followers, and all the friends, family and colleagues who compose the Communities of our days. Christ in our

Community is in all of these. We extend His Love into every heart of every person we meet, into every encounter that comes in our path, and into every word in all our conversations. There is no limitation to the amount of this Love we can extend—we just have to be aware this is our main function in Life. What better job would we have to do?

We stand together, Christ and I, in peace and certainty of purpose. In him is His creator, as He is in me. *(ACIM; Workbook; Lesson # 354)*

What would "standing together" with Christ mean for you? We would have to be serious to stand with Christ. It is not something to be taken lightly. It is not a partial commitment we would make on Sundays but forget about it for the rest of the week. At the same time, it is a Joyous commitment, not something heavy and with struggle. We are asked to embrace our holiness, our innocence, our perfect happiness, our urge to have something to give. These are the best aspects of ourselves. *Standing together* with Christ means to stand as the True Self we are. When we are doing that we are a blessing to our Community, in whatever way, shape or form that Community takes on to receive our blessing.

Tara Singh encouraged us to have a "service project" to which we devoted some of our time. He spoke of the "joy of service" through having something to give. So, for three years I helped weekly in a Mother Teresa Mission in their soup kitchen. I also did some building projects for the Sisters in their facility. This work for the Community was packed full of lessons. The first was learning that one should not expect any gratitude in return from people you are serving. The poor and the homeless are that way for the very reason they lack gratitude—so they are not so capable of being thankful. However, the Sisters had a plaque in the kitchen that said: "what a privilege it was to serve." The action of serving is already the reward, inherent in it. That began to make sense.

I would go with some other fellow students of *A Course in Miracles* to help out in whatever ways were needed. Sometimes we would go very early and say morning prayers with the Sisters. They were so pure. They were so Joyous. They had stepped into another dimension of togetherness in which their faith and their purpose were joined with the Christ. I would say they "stood together with Him," and this was their deep inner truth—it was not just a belief or an intellectual exercise of "social work."

Now our community is different, and it is worldwide. It is our Community of readers, seminar organizers, fellow Liberation Breathing Practitioners, our clients and students, and our friends.

I am among the ministers of God.
(ACIM; Workbook; Lesson #154)

What is that ministry? I said above it is your email contacts and your Facebook friends. But it is more than that even. Your ministry has a great purpose in your Community. Your main ministry is to end the separation you feel, and the division you still made between you and the Christ Self. The Christ Self is in you. You are the Christ. Tara Singh made this very clear to us in various talks he gave at his *Foundation for Life Action.*

> *If you stayed with It, you could come to It [the Christ] that extends, and It is not you [your ego]. Then would you want to change It? As long as you are going to see It through words, then It is regulated by words. So, That is no understanding at all; then you will want the "opposite." And therefore I clear the way, and don't accept those [conclusions] as real—and I have to come to awareness. Awareness would see them [thoughts] not as real. And somewhere this awareness intensifies, to the degree that no thought manipulates it. And then if you are really sincere, probably you would come upon Life Itself that extends. And there is nothing you can do about it. You are blessed if you will not*

make it personal. Your life is alive, and it extends. But if I am afraid, and I hate somebody else, then I am not going to go the extension way. Then I live in the man-made world, the man-projected world. So, are we going to come to that intensity? What discipline it would require, of being watchful, that's all.

(Tara Singh, from the lectures, "What is the Christ?" Lecture #1)

I was fortunate to have Tara Singh's wisdom around me for seventeen years. Many a lecture would I be sitting at his feet, in the front row, absorbing his true words into me, and endeavoring to the best of my ability to bring the true words he was speaking into application in my life.

Christ in our community is no less than receiving the Christ in ourselves, and then—being THAT within our community. It begins with the individual, extending "small acts of Love," wherever you are because that is natural and the right thing to do. One does not effort or "learn" to do this. Once the subterfuge of the ego thought is removed, what extends is the "stillness of the peace of God." One does everything with an awareness of attention that is thorough and necessary. There are then no "wasted motions" in life, and everything one does is purposeful. Christ in the community is the ultimate "just being our real Self."

20. Christ in Our Relationship

The fragrance of a Holy relationship fills our life with the sweet aromas of a living breath of Immortal Joy. The unholy or "special" relationship brings with it the stench of discontent, disharmony, disease, decay, and death. The choice is always ours to establish the purpose and means of any relationship, having the free will to do so. Are we in a Holy Relationship or an unholy one?

I had my first Holy Relationship with Tara Singh, whom I met in 1989. Up until that year, I would have thought that twelve years of marriage would have produced a Holy Relationship between my ex-wife and me. We were both looking toward the sacred to encompass and surround our life as artists, but the struggles of daily life (and survival of our artistic callings) absorbed much of our attention. There were good times and difficult times as most couples have. I did not stop to question, "there must be another way." Until I met Tara Singh, that is.

The first thing Tara Singh said when I met him at an Easter Retreat in Stony Point, New York, was, "I have nothing to teach. You know too much already." I was shocked. What would he say for the rest of the weekend? He continued to point out, "You all have learned too much already. You have learned to be insecure. You have learned to be fearful. You have learned to be greedy and self-centered." One could not argue with what he was saying, as they were actual states of the human mind and condition. It became more and more clear why he "had nothing to teach." In other words, he had nothing to add to the accumulations of "knowledge" we had put together to define our personal "self." We had all made up a *polite hell*, while pretending it was otherwise.

There is wisdom in "undoing." Tara Singh called this the "love of correction." It was a process of dismantling the "self I made up." One could be frightened by this process, as we have fought long and hard to construct this "self." There is a lot of resistance to letting it go. But the more I read *A Course in Miracles* and got the principles it was putting forth, the more I saw Tara Singh was actualizing the lessons in his relationship with his students—mainly with me! He was the great liberator of thought itself. He was the destroyer of illusions. He was willing to confront my ego at its root level, and this made the ego's deceptions so clear I had to drop them. And what was left in the space was an incredible stillness and silence. What was left in the space was my true Self of the Peace of God.

What is the best way to be free of the past, and then have a meeting with you in the present? You are reading this book, and I owe it to you, my reader, to give you the same stillness and silence given to me by my teacher, Tara Singh. Otherwise, why waste our time? The relationship we have, established by you picking up this book, and reading this far, is a Holy one. The title is *The Second Coming: You Are the Christ*. Okay, you might ask, "Prove it."

We all seem caught in a variety of circumstances. But this Holy Instant is the same for all—can we drop everything from the past, even drop these circumstances—good, bad, or indifferent—to meet together in this present moment? In this meeting is the Second Coming. We must be completely honest with each other. There is nothing we are trying to hide. We are taking full responsibility for our life. We have transcended being a "victim" of anything, including our own opinions and thought processes. We come to meet each other in this empty space. There is no "project" to accomplish, and nothing to learn. We meet "to Be," and nothing more than that. But also, nothing less than that. To Be is the greatest realization we could have. We are as God created us now. This Identity does not require improvement or self-developing of any kind. It already is inherently inside of us. It just needs to be awakened. And for that, we merely remove what is not our true Self. This is what Jesus calls "removing the blocks to the awareness of Love's presence."

> *The course does not aim at teaching the meaning of love, for that is beyond what can be taught. It does aim, however, at* ***removing the blocks to the awareness of love's presence****, which is your natural inheritance.*
> *(ACIM; Text; Intro)*

Any commentary on awakening to our true Self would have to begin with removing the parts of our mind which keep us asleep. Love cannot be taught. But it can be awakened. Something we did not know was Love can only be seen when we let go of what we think is there, which is blocking our view of it. Love, in this case, has been obscured from our view by parts of our mind—fear, anger, judgment, grievances, dwelling on negative feelings, jealousy, attachment, undue pride, lust, inferiority or superiority. These compose the false self of the ego which must be "undone" first.

This can happen in an instant, but most of us seem to need time to let go of our false self we made up. We come face to face with what Tara Singh called our main block—the *unwillingness* to let go, to change, to admit we have made up a false self. Unwillingness maintains the sleep we are in. We cannot wake up to the stillness of the Peace of God without facing and overcoming in ourselves this inherent unwillingness.

> ***The sleep of forgetfulness is only the unwillingness to remember Your forgiveness and Your Love.***
> *(ACIM; Text; Chapter 17; Section VII)*

The "sleep of forgetfulness" is the status quo of our unwillingness in our life to remember the most important relationship—the one with our Divinity. We are given *A Course in Miracles* to help us wake up from this sleep and to remember God within our Divine nature. In this real nature, there is nothing to add, nothing to subtract. It is perfect already, just the way it is. But we may think we need to educate ourselves on it. We should have a Ph.D. in self-identity. That's like telling the apple tree it needs to take a college course to learn how to produce apples. The forgiveness and Love of God are planted in us already. It is the Love of God that awakens, and the gift of forgiveness that erases all the consequences of our mistakes. It is the Christ in us Who completes our awakening, and until we can do this for ourselves, the Teacher is here to help us remove our self-deceptions.

What woke me up was a direct relationship with a real teacher who was not going to feed me a bunch of self-improvement baloney. He did not distract me into more techniques or things I needed to learn. He met me head-on in the moment of my Divine perfection. He saw my God created Self, even in the times I did not see it. He questioned my ego to the point of excruciating self-honesty. He undid the most stubborn blind spots in my psyche. He Loved me beyond my reason. Tara Singh was the Christ in my Relationship to Life. He was the Light that shined away the doubt lodged in the doldrums of my stubborn unwillingness. He was my savior for a day and every day to this day. He was my everything.

The blessings of Life are realized in the Holy Relationship. Once you find it once, you can transfer its unfathomable Joy to every one of the Relationships in your Life. It is an undeniable boon placed in the store of your perfect happiness by a benevolent and compassionate Creator. It cannot be fathomed in words that are mere reflections of truth. It cannot be sought in sensations that are replicas of this totality of purpose. It cannot be expressed—this contact that ascends above all other human experiences. My Holy relationship with Tara Singh was the greatest blessing life could bestow. You can read more about it here: *Miracles with My Master, Tara Singh* (bit.ly/TSRay)

You may like to pursue our relationship further. You can do this by joining *Miracles for You: A 1-Year Support Network for Serious Study of A Course in Miracles*. (bit.ly/Miracles4You) This is an online study group with daily postings and a Q&A forum. What I found was the holy Relationship spoken of in *A Course in Miracles* needed to be actual in my life. My relationship with Tara Singh made manifest what could very easily have been left as a theory. No theory was possible around this teacher. If it was not your truth from your contact and experience, then it was abstract speculation—and just more of "meaningless thought." Tara Singh met me in the Present in every encounter I had with him. This was confronting and exhilarating at the same time. But it was the crucible in which the fire of transformation burned most brightly. I threw myself into it to have my ego incinerated.

I invite you into this crucible of the Holy Relationship. There is nothing else comparable in Life. When Christ has entered our Relationship we embark on a journey to realize our true destiny—and overcome all tattered remnants of unwillingness in us. We seek to reach the Truth—together.

> ***No one can fail who seeks to reach the truth.***
> *(ACIM; Workbook; Lesson #131)*

PART 5

We Are the Christ

21. Undoing Our Personal Lies

The nature of thought is imbued with opposites. These opposites seem natural—up and down; light and dark; good and evil; slow and fast; desirable and undesirable—and the ultimate opposite, Life and Death. The world of our thought applied to ourselves does not escape this dichotomy of opposing forces. Therefore, the negative and positive aspects of our soul seem equally real. Our self-identity seems malleable between reconciling ourselves amidst these opposing positions. Sometimes we feel strong. Yet, at other times we feel weak. Today we may be living demonstrably in an action of great passion—and tomorrow we may be dead. Life and Death are the ultimate dualities of a system in which we feel somewhat trapped. Did we ever stop to question the reality of "opposites?" Did we ever stop to question the power and belief in the inevitability of "death?" We are doing this now, right here. Is it possible to step entirely outside of the known? Is it possible to have no negative thoughts about ourselves? Is it possible to have immortality in the flesh? And this would amount to living our life with a mind not governed by relative thought. This would amount to stepping totally outside the realm of opposites. It becomes a matter of even changing our DNA—the DNA from the relative thoughts and memories of our ancestors to the DNA from the Absolute Thoughts of God.

This is a major reboot of our mind, all the way down to the cellular level in our bodies. It is a kind of transmutation the likes of which few have ever gone through. It is a shift from the limitations of mortality to the unlimited possibilities of the Immortal. It is like nothing we have ever experienced, nor is there a scientific "method" by which we can construct or facilitate this "shift." We could say it requires "faith" or even the trust that such a shift is possible. But even this is nearly unreachable with the realms of the mind we use in everyday life. It is going beyond our "comfort zone" into the Unknown Zone of God and Divine Will.

Truth will correct all errors in my mind.
(ACIM; Workbook; Lesson #107)

What are the errors? They would have to be "untruths." In other words, they are "lies" we hold about ourselves and the world. We need to be liberated from these lies, but the problem is we do not fully realize we even have them. They are lodged in our subconscious mind which conceals them in a smokescreen of undeclared acceptance. We wrote an entire book about the "Personal Lie," and how to be free from this biggest block to Pure Joy. It is called *Liberation: Freedom from Your Biggest Block to Pure Joy.* (bit.ly/LibRay)

A "Personal Lie" is your most dominant subconscious negative thought about yourself. Common ones are "I am not good enough," "I am wrong," "I am bad," "I am a failure," "I am not perfect," or "I am guilty." Everyone has one of these thoughts. This thought is at the root of our darkest side of personal shadows. People sometimes deny that they even have one, especially very successful people in the world. The thought can be shrouded in a whole persona of overcompensation. One with a thought, "I am not good enough," can seek the approval of millions of fans. Some famous entertainers have even confessed that they needed the approval of their fans to feel the least bit "good enough." And when their ratings plummeted, they would be back in the doldrums of their insecurities.

Someone who is constantly coming up short in life could have the subconscious thought, "I am a failure." This thought sabotages everything they touch until they own it, and unravel the memories of its effects from their mind. This amounts to radical forgiveness of their whole personal self, and a break from their past. Freedom from this debilitating "Personal Lie" is one of the major functions of any spiritual work. It is essentially seeing the whole content of the mind contains these negative thoughts because it is inherently a dualistic system—and through a kind of renunciation, or radical forgiveness, to step outside of this system altogether. This is the Miracle of Truth to which *A Course in Miracles* is leading us. This is the "Truth" that can "correct all errors in my mind."

We are given a hint of what this Freedom would be like. It refers to these lies as "illusions." A completely forgiven world would look like this:

> *Can you imagine what a state of mind without illusions is? How it would feel? Try to remember when there was a time,—perhaps a minute, maybe even less—when nothing came to interrupt your peace; when you were certain you were loved and safe. Then try to picture what it would be like to have that moment be extended to the end of time and to eternity. Then let the sense of quiet that you felt be multiplied a hundred times, and then be multiplied another hundred more. (ACIM; Workbook; Lesson #107)*

We are looking here at a state of Mind that is Absolute. It is not racked with the conflicts of opposites, but rather in a total state of inner peace. Have we ever stepped out of the thought system we have made to embrace the Thought System God created? This is the radical shift in perspective needed to replace our ancestral DNA with God's DNA. DNA is merely a "structure of memory" at the cellular level. And this "remembrance" of our Perfection, our Immortality, our Divine Connection, is the only rightful use of memory. All other uses which contain even the slightest specter of disease, sorrow, and death are to be transcended in this spiritual work we do.

Try to remember when there was a time,—perhaps a minute, maybe even less—when nothing came to interrupt your peace; when you were certain you were loved and safe. Then try to picture what it would be like to have that moment be extended to the end of time and to eternity. *(ACIM; Workbook; Lesson #107)*

This is not a "Personal Lie" of not feeling good enough or being in perpetual conflict with ourselves. This is a God Created State of Being in which we were originally created. It is an Eternal State of Pure Joy! Wouldn't we all like this awareness restored to our Minds right now? Why delay. Why waste time in dreams of sorrow or death? We must claim this state of Mind as our natural inheritance. Yet, this requires first that we drop the content of our thought we have made up and accumulated.

In the beginning ten lessons of *A Course in Miracles*, if we are bringing them into application in our life, this dismantling of our mind is taking place. "Nothing I see means anything." "I do not understand anything I see." "I see nothing as it is now." "My thoughts do not mean anything." Who has done this work of "undoing?" We must master these beginning lessons and step out of the thought system we made up. Can we do it? Can we let go of all the opinions, goals and memories lodged in our personal life?

God did not create us with any limitations. We made them up ourselves in an imagined "separation from our Source." The "Personal Lie" is the main way we maintain this sense of separation. Here is a process we created to help you free yourself from your "Personal Lie." Let's use a common one, "I am bad," for demonstration purposes:

1. I forgive myself for ever thinking, "I am bad."
2. God did not create me with the thought, "I am bad."
3. God created me good.
4. I am as God created me.
5. Therefore, that thought, "I am bad," is a lie.
6. I let go of my stubborn refusal to release that thought.
7. I ask the Holy Spirit to help me let that thought go.
8. My eternal Truth is that I am good.

It sounds too simple, but we have to undo and redo our mind with some kind of reversal of our "Personal Lie." Without giving some attention to make this shift—which amounts to no less than invoking God's Power of the Holy Spirit to help us—our minds will stay stuck in the duality of deep subconscious conflict.

This shift is instantaneous. One does not have to struggle or "work hard" to release the personal DNA of relative thought for the Divine DNA of our Absolute Thought. Every time we choose JOY over the problems and quagmires of personal troubles, we make huge leaps in this shift of consciousness and awareness of our True Self. The true state of Mind is problem-free. Totally. Only the ego can have problems. The God-created Self does not have problems of any kind. It is our determination, then, to "undo" all of the parts of ourselves that are false and "untrue." We further this action more by choosing thoughts, feelings, and situations that reinforce our feelings of Joy and general well-being. The choice is ours because we have dominion over the attention of our Minds. We can just as easily focus on Heaven as we can on hell.

22. Physical Immortality

Life and Death are functions of the mind. As we just discussed, there is a mind of the ego which is immersed in "opposites," giving equal validity to these opposites; and there is an Absolute Thought System, we could call it the *Mind of God*, which has transcended all opposites and sees the Oneness of all Creation. We could also call these two very different "minds" the "mortal mind" and the "Immortal Mind."

As a function of the mind, we all possess what is called in breathwork "an unconscious death urge." What exactly is this? In general, it is a collection of all your negative thoughts and "death programming" inherited from your family, your society, and your memories of incarnating and dying in the end. Specifically, it is your "Personal Lie," your belief that you are separate from the Life Force (God), and your belief that "death is inevitable." These are all thoughts that can be changed.

I rule my mind, which I alone must rule.
(ACIM; Workbook; Lesson # 236)

You have dominion over your mind, which is a collection of thoughts. You have limiting and debilitating negative thoughts of the ego; and you have expansive, timeless, and unlimited Thoughts of your Creator. You always have a choice of what you will put into your mind, and what you will take out of it.

I must stress, and stress again and again, "Thought always precedes form." Physical manifestation does not happen without a thought or series of thoughts that come before it. This applies even to "death." There is no entropic law of the Universe that says all things must die. No rule says you have only so many "breaths" before you "kick the bucket" in a kind of "pre-determined" number of days to live. Sickness, disease, and death are brought about by thoughts. They may be deeply submerged in the subconscious, and you may not be aware of them, but they are there—manifesting themselves in formal compliance. Until you clear them, they will be killing you in a slow march to the grave.

You may say, "How do I clear myself of the unconscious death urge?" This is a good question. But it starts with your willingness to completely give up your affiliation to the three main "killers:" 1) Your "Personal Lie," 2) Your belief in Separation, 3) Your belief that "death is inevitable." If you are willing to divorce yourself from these "thought forms," then you have a chance to conquer death. Otherwise, you will reap what you sow, and you are sowing the seeds of death unaware. Then when death and disease come closer, you will have no history of questioning their hold, and it will be "too late."

So let's undo them right here and now—one at a time. We talked in the previous Chapter about the "Personal Lie." It is a result of dualistic "thinking," and relative thought of opposites that says, "Both opposites are true." In this thought system, both "life and death" are equally "true." And it is based on putting physical demonstration ahead of the preceding thought. "I know I am a failure because I had three businesses that failed," or I "flunked out" of three colleges." Or "I know I am bad because I was caught stealing something from the local grocery store when I was a kid, and I was severely punished by my parents." In these cases, both "failure or success" or being "bad or good" seem like equal "truths." And then we are caught in an endless struggle between the two possibilities.

In an Absolute thought system, only one is Created—only one is True. The seeming "opposite" is made as a contrast, but because it was not created in tandem with the Universal Laws of the Life Force, it is not "true," and therefore it does not really exist. Even from a mental aspect, we have to see we "rule our mind," and the thought "I am a failure" was a choice we made long before we "flunked out of school" or "had a business that failed." These were "results," not "causes." And because there is only one true Cause—call it the Life Force, or the Universal Divine Energy, and its Nature is Pure Joy and the endless manifestation of this Joy, this Unity, this Wholeness—then anything that introduces division, fragmentation, and conflict is by its very nature false.

God Created me Good. God created me consistent with my function, therefore always a success. God created me immortal. And the "opposites" of these states are only my "projections." The unconscious death urge is dismantled when I see this fundamental nature of the Unity of the Life Force. Love is whole and all-inclusive. It is Immortal and never-ending. Therefore Love does not have "death" in its field of being. When we identify with Love we eliminate "death" from our field of Being as well.

Now let's look at our sense of "separation" from the Life Force. We are not so keen on the word God this day and age. Too much has come down from the debilitating dogmas of organized religions around the world that have kept mankind in "bondage," rather than freeing people from these church laws, rules, and moral condemnations. We stepped out of this many years ago. But, the Life Force remains, regardless of the false theologies of organized religions that maintain the duality of good and evil, believers and unbelievers, the saved and the damned, and then promote the belief in the duality of Life and Death itself. God does not create "organized religions." Man makes them up in his deep sense of separation from his Source Energy. If he had this Divine Connection already inside of himself, what need does he have for such things? Not much. He would be walking and breathing and acting in the glory of this Holy Communion with God all of the time—every second of his day. Holy Communion is not a sacrament dished out to some and not to others, only on special occasions. Holy Communion is the birthright of every man, woman, and child on the planet—and every animal, every particle of dust, every drop of water in the ocean, every sacred element making up the entire Cosmos. Every breath we take is a Holy Communion. There is nothing that is not in Holy Communion with its Creator all of the time. So this is what I mean about ending the "separation" we feel from our Source Energy—with life itself. Healing this, we see we are at ONE with everything—with the sun, the moon and the stars! We are in Communion with every living creature; with all the elements that extend to the far reaches of the Cosmos. With every breath, we are affirming the Holy Life Force of being here in this present moment of *infinite now.*

A mind free of negative, limiting thoughts—and connected with certainty to this Life Force—transcends the dualistic mind. In this Mind, there is no "death." It has transcended even its identification with the body. The body is seen as a tool of expression in this physical dimension. But the Mind Identifies with Spirit. By doing so, the Mind is liberated from lower orders and concerns and enters a "carefree" state. Even the health of the body is improved in this Identification. Because the purpose of the Mind is to realize and communicate its Freedom, its Innocence, and its Pure Joy—and it needs a body to do this. The body, then, is a communication device in the service of the Mind which Identifies with Love. There is no other purpose for the Body, except to express this Divine Connection, this Divine Bliss of Pure Being.

Physical Immortality is the ability to live in the body, in a state of good health, for as long as you choose. This could be well over 100 years old, and even beyond that. People in the Bible were said to have lived 800 years, 900 years, etc. Melchizedek, purported to have not been born of a woman, like Babaji, was ageless. One could dismiss these claims as mere myths, or one could consider another mindset in which Divine Will has transcendence over the definitions and limitations we have placed on Life. What we would benefit from most is to dismiss the evidence we seek to formulate our "scientific proof" to support these limitations. Maybe no person we have met in this lifetime has transcended the "unconscious death urge," so we might say this is crazy, wishful fantasy. But people died from their own thoughts. All disease is preceded by negative thoughts. Therefore, examination and release of negative thoughts would have a direct effect on the health, well-being, and life extension of the body—which are all ruled by the Mind.

Here is a thought you may have a hard time accepting, but which is profoundly true:

> ***There is no Death. The Son of God is free.*** *It is impossible to worship death in any form, and still select a few you would not cherish and would yet avoid, while still believing in the rest. For death is total. Either all things die, or else they live and cannot die. No compromise is possible. For here again we see an obvious position, which we must accept if we be sane; what contradicts one thought entirely cannot be true, unless its opposite is proven false. (ACIM; Workbook; Lesson #163)*

For "death" to be true we would have to prove "life" false. And this is what we are trying to do with our *unconscious death urge.* What this amounts to is we are "living dead," not fully awakened to the Immortal Life we are. Who would accept this premise as true? It has made us angry. We feel abandoned by God. We need to make a different choice, one in which our own demise is not "inevitable." "No compromise is possible" in our choice for Immortal Life. Life is Immortal, or it is racked with a condition that negates it. Some may say, "I know death is inevitable, because I see all these people dying out there." Well, people are dying out there because they did not change their thought, "Death is inevitable." Their thoughts preceded their results and "killed them" in the end.

We have written a whole book on this one subject: *Physical Immortality: How To Overcome Death*. You can order it here: (bit.ly/ImmortalRay). Basically, Immortal Life is a matter of making a decision. One must first decide it is a viable possibility; then one must embrace the Philosophy of it, the Psychology of it, and the Physiology of it. The Philosophy of it is to immerse yourself in the literature out there, starting with our book and others. Next, the Psychology of it is to unravel your "unconscious death urge" through breathwork and study of *A Course in Miracles*. And thirdly, The Physiology of it is to study and discover how your body is an energy system affected by your thoughts, your attention, your diet, and your beliefs. Body mastery is part of Physical Immortality. And these three areas are an ongoing study and practice. There are other factors as well—right work; right livelihood; right relationships; right attitudes. And we also say it is necessary to embrace the Divine Mother Energy. She is the creator of the Physical Universe, so the right relationship with the Divine Mother is a must. In India, the wise say, "only the Divine Mother grants the boon of Physical Immortality." That statement alone would inspire one to have a whole different outlook on a Holy Relationship.

Being the Christ includes embracing Immortality, not only of the Spirit, but of our whole Being who makes decisions in this dimension of what, where, how long, and why we live on this planet as our true Self.

23.
The End of Sickness

What would you do if you knew all sickness is a result of the wrong thoughts? Would you want to change them? Would you decide to "get up off your sickbed and walk?" Would you say that is impossible? Would you be in fear that "you are never going to get over this?" When we are in a state of sickness, we do not usually look at the "mental factors" involved in manifesting the sickness in the first place. Memories and conditions are stored in the subconscious mind; and when sickness comes along, we don't usually make the connection that these memories are just activated and replaying again, in slightly different forms.

A traumatic experience from the past leaves its scar. This usually comes with a complex of judgments about people, places and things, including judgments about ourselves. We form opinions about our life based on these memories. How we feel in the moment is often tainted by these opinions and mental patterns put in us from our family and early life experiences. A complete break from the ties of the past is seldom accomplished without an extended process of introspection and forgiveness. We tend to hold *grievances*, and *thoughts of unforgiveness*. This complex of subtle (and sometimes not so subtle) "blame" keeps us in a state of "victim consciousness." This is an insistence that things are "done to us," and we are subject to acts and circumstances beyond our control. "Shit happens" is the common statement of this uncontrollable fate of negative encounters. When negative experiences happen, we seldom ask, "What were the thoughts and feelings in me which attracted this experience." If we do not process these experiences in some way of self-responsibility, then we would remain to feel and be a victim. This negative feeling that harbors guilt is at the root of all disease and suffering. All bodily "ills" are results of mental guilts, grievances, attacks, and limitations.

Sickness is a defense against the truth.
(ACIM; Workbook; Lesson #136)

What would the truth be, then? God's peace and joy are ours to claim, but certainly, sickness and negative thoughts would block us from receiving this inheritance. How does sickness arise? How does it block the truth? And once we are in some sort of sickness, what is the best way to heal ourselves and get out of it? Man has grappled with these questions from time immemorial. We are beginning to see that the modern medical model of procedures and pharmaceuticals does not necessarily provide the cure for our illnesses. Often this model is one of "disease management" that ends in a slow decline of the body toward an "inevitable" demise of death. Is it possible to heal the sickness at the root cause, which has little to do with the body, per se, and everything to do with the attention of the mind?

We would do well to consider *truth*, and what Jesus means by the *truth*. He is certainly talking about an Absolute Truth that does not alter or change. He is certainly talking about a Truth that dispels the false. He is certainly talking about a state of Being in which only the Truth is true—and the false, being false, does not really exist. I would liken the false to a kind of mirage: it is something which only appears to be real, but upon closer examination, it does not exist at all. Though we seem to "see it" with the body's eyes, it disappears into the ethers of wishful hallucination.

When it comes to the body, and what we deem as "physical sickness," the mind is distracted in believing something that is not "true" in the higher levels of Being. In these higher levels of Being, sickness does not exist. The negative thoughts and feelings that we keep thinking and feeling can manifest in the body as particular disease. But the thoughts and feelings preceding the manifestation of sickness are not true. Positive thoughts and feelings that produce Peace and Joy are True. These are in alignment with our Source, God, Divine Energy, Infinite Intelligence, Creative Reality, or whatever you want to call That Life Force from Which we originate. Sickness, which manifests from us trying to maintain a separation from Truth with the falsity of negative thoughts and feelings—anger, resentment, disappointment, jealousy, envy, lack, loneliness, etc.—is, therefore, a *defense against the Truth* of Peace and Joy.

OK, many of us may find ourselves in the middle of some chronic dis-ease in the body. What do we do? Forgive ourselves at once for this mistake. Ask ourselves what the negative thought factors were that contributed to the manifestation of the disease; then give attention to the corrections of these thoughts and feelings in our mind and everyday life. Reach for a higher thought, a better feeling, and greater gratitude for all that is given in our life already. Are we going to focus on the 1% that may not be working in our life or the 99% that's going very well and gives us cause for happiness? This is always up to us. We have dominion over our thoughts and feelings. I can feel glad now to know that I am good enough even if I felt sad in the past from thinking I was "not good enough." The beginning of healing a chronic ailment is changing the causative factors of thoughts and feelings.

The best book of reference for the thoughts and feelings that cause diseases is by Dr. Michael Lincoln, Ph.D., called *Messages From The Body*. He lists almost every bodily ailment you could think of, and then goes into the psychological and familial causes of that disease. This book is ten times more thorough than other "new age" books out there by more "popular" authors. You can heal your life by looking at the nitty-gritty of the most negative thought structures that made up physical disease, and then you need to shift your focus immediately away from these "causes." They still will amount to "defenses against the truth." The Truth leads us into thoughts and feelings of higher vibrations. We want to feel good, not bad; we want to be healthy and well, not sick and diseased.

As the channel for Abraham, Esther Hicks would say that dwelling on the negative factors in your life will only give you more of their negative experiences, which are a "vibrational match" to them. We have to shift our focus into the feelings of gratitude and joy if we are to heal ourselves and rise above the "contrast" between what we want and what we may be experiencing of "not having," such as good health. There are seven lessons in *A Course in Miracles* that make the direction clear:

1. ***God's Will for me is perfect happiness.*** *(Which is also perfect health.) ACIM, Lesson #101*

2. ***I share God's will for happiness for me.*** *ACIM, Lesson #102*

3. ***I seek but what belongs to me in truth***. *Lesson #104*

4. ***God's Peace and Joy are mine****. ACIM, Lesson #105*

5. ***I will be still and listen to the truth****. ACIM, Lesson #106*

6. ***Truth will correct all errors in my mind.*** *ACIM, Lesson #107*

7. ***To give and to receive are one in truth****, ACIM Lesson #108*

Let's look at these lessons more carefully now to help us undo any chronic disease we may have.

God's will for us is "perfect happiness." Perfect happiness does not include disease, wouldn't we all agree? Therefore, sickness must not be God's will for us. God gives us the Truth of perfect happiness, so if we are not in a state of perfect happiness, then we must be "separated" from God's will with a "false will" of our own.

This "will" from our Creator must be shared. By accepting and sharing in it, we are reinforcing the truth of "perfect happiness" within ourselves, and with the people who receive our perfect happiness. Did you notice how a happy person will lift the spirits of other people in the room? We extend what we share in ourselves and with others. If we share in the doldrums, we just get more of that—depression and bad feelings. If we share in peace and joy and gratitude, we and all the people around us rise into a higher state of that.

We are seeking the truth. We are seeking perfect health that goes along with perfect happiness. We are seeking to turn around any negative feelings and experiences in our vibrational field even now—right now. Whatever you and I are experiencing right now that may be negative, we seek to let it go and bask in the Truth. We want the Truth. We no longer want to "defend against it." We will not dwell on the sickness but on the health of who we are as God created us to be. We will not fall into a depression about our "chronic illness," but stay in a state of joy that it can be healed in us.

"God's Peace and Joy are mine." This is such a simple statement of the Truth, but we have to claim it. We have to let go and let this Peace and Joy arise in us. It is a meditation in the Truth when we are happy. What makes us feel good is a Joy and a Peace that comes into our awareness, our focus of attention, from a place on High. We are talking about Universal Peace and Joy now, not the flimsy peace that is man-made, which can turn just as easily into a world war. We are talking about Absolute Peace and Joy. Who has made contact with this? This is what heals. This is what will heal the "sickness that is a defense against the truth."

But for this Peace and Joy of God to be truly heard by us, we have to listen to it. And what we will find is all our thoughts of conflict, judgment, grievances, that separate us from the Truth. We have a responsibility to "still our mind," to forgive all of those with whom we hold grievances and to empty our thoughts to receive God's Thoughts of Truth. Everyone can do this, but who will decide to do it? Who will see their sinlessness—their guiltlessness—and the innocence of all others as well? This is what is required to "be still and listen to the truth."

It is a great boon from the Divine when we do this. Jesus assures us, "Truth will correct all errors in my mind." Well, sickness is an error. We have to see it this way. Not in a way in which we feel worse for our mistake, or guilty that we "made up a disease" that seems to have the better of us. Can we, together here now, look at all the feelings in ourselves, and manifested in our bodies that do not instill perfect happiness? Can we look at them together now and forgive ourselves for them? We can. We can "be still and listen to the truth" of our innocence, even amidst these mistakes we may have made. We can listen to the truth even amidst any discomfort or pain we may be feeling now.

Together we invite the Holy Spirit to undo our fear, our resentment, our anger, our distrust that may have thrown us into a disease. We ask the Holy Spirit to restore us to Peace and Joy, essentially to the Love Who we are. We receive this Love from the Holy Spirit, and we "give it out" to share and increase it. Any grievances we hold toward ourselves or others we drop them now. We let go of feelings of unhappiness for the hope, for the trust, for the certainty that God will respond to our call, and honor our action of forgiveness that we undertake. We are responsible now, for all that has happened to us. We forgive ourselves completely for all our "defenses against the truth," and now accept the pure and simple truth of our perfect happiness, God's Peace and Joy that are ours.

What we give out we will receive. What we extend is a part of us. We Claim the healing now. We put ourselves in the trust that we can be better. We can be healed and whole. We are already healed and whole, even amidst the residue of symptoms lingering in the body. We are willing to "fast" from the indulgences of negative thoughts and feelings. And in this fast, we are cleansing ourselves of fear and suffering. We are willing to embrace the Truth. This is our Self of perfection that is already here, already ours to use in our rejoicing. The End of sickness is upon us because we are no longer defending against real health, which is the truth of God's will for us to have perfect happiness, now and forever.

24. The Grandeur of Resurrection

The theme of resurrection is not new. Ancient cultures honored the new life of Spring and the end of the Winter cycle which appeared to bring the frigid culmination of the harvest months to a kind of suspended animation, a frozen ground of death that held life in abeyance for a season. It is a rising from the dead. We are all well versed in the story of Jesus's resurrection. He gave miraculous healings and speeches to the public for a few years, and at the close of His mission was crucified by the Roman administration (by request of the Jewish Sanhedrin). On the 3rd day after His death, He rose from the dead, thus culminating the highest act of supernatural prowess yet know to mankind.

One could believe this to be a myth—or accept it as the Good News of a Truth that sets the Christ at the pinnacle of human evolution. But even mythology offers us a metaphysical logic of the human psyche that attests to the heroic aspects of our soul in its ascent toward attaining immortality. The Second Coming of Christ offers us, in the form of *A Course in Miracles,* the correction of all errors (the Atonement) through complete forgiveness. The attainment of Absolute Love is the goal of our True Identity. Christ is the catalyst for this quantum leap in our evolution, particularly referred to in the *Course* as our "Salvation." The Atonement is made possible through the Resurrection—our resurrection is an awakening out of the separated "self" we made into the awareness of the Unified Self Who God created.

> *The crucifixion did not establish the Atonement; the resurrection did. Many sincere Christians have misunderstood this. No one who is free of the belief in scarcity could possibly make this mistake. (ACIM; Text; Chapter 3; Section I; ¶1)*

Why did the resurrection establish Christ's importance as a spiritual figure in the history of human spiritual development? What allowed Him to be able to resurrect from the dead in the first place?

Christ did not "die for our sins." His death on the cross was a teaching opportunity He took on to prove there are no victims, and even attack as severe as this did not merit "counter-attack" from Him toward His attackers of any kind.

> *Miracle-minded forgiveness is* only *correction. It has no element of judgment at all. The statement "Father forgive them for they know not what they do" in no way evaluates* what *they do. It is an appeal to God to heal their minds. There is no reference to the outcome of the error. That does not matter.*
> *(ACIM; Text; Chapter 2; Section V; ¶1)*

In other words, He did not "sacrifice" Himself to pay for our mistakes. He demonstrated to us that no "mistake," even in the case of someone else's attack on us, has any real effect on our Divine Being—unless we judge it to affect us. And because He did not judge it and forgave his "attackers" completely, He was able to resurrect Himself from the dead. Resurrection is the ultimate awakening into the Self God created us to be:

> *The resurrection is the complete triumph of Christ over the ego, not by attack but by transcendence. For Christ does rise above the ego and all its works, and ascends to the Father and His Kingdom— Would you join in the resurrection or the crucifixion? Would you condemn your brothers or free them? Would you transcend your prison and ascend to the Father? These questions are all the same, and are answered together.*
> *(ACIM; Text; Chapter 11; Section IV; ¶1-2)*

We must place the ego in the service to our Higher Self. This is the Self of Peace and Joy as we learned in the former chapter. It is the Self who has transcended problems and even disease and lives in communion with the inner Christ all of the time. As long as we are in a body, in physical existence, we will have an "ego." Yet the collection of thoughts that make up the "ego's rule" over us is dismantled by the miracles pouring forth from the Christ. This transformation is in us. We witness it taking place through our willingness to change our mind, and think a different Thought which is not subject to limitations, judgments, and errors of replayed memories from our painful past.

I choose the joy of God instead of pain.
(ACIM; Workbook; Lesson #190)

We are given an opportunity in this dimension to choose joy over pain, light over darkness, truth over illusion, and Heaven over hell. Ultimately this amounts to choosing Life over death. It sounds too simple, doesn't it? But it is a simple decision when we realize that it is our thoughts and feelings which determine whether we experience pain and suffering. Pain is preceded by some thought of guilt or attack that we are clinging to with power:

> *It is your thoughts alone that cause you pain. Nothing external to your mind can hurt or injure you in any way. There is no cause beyond yourself that can reach down and bring oppression. No one but yourself affects you. There is nothing in the world that has the power to make you ill or sad, or weak or frail. But it is you who have the power to dominate all things you see by merely recognizing what you are. As you perceive the harmlessness in them, they will accept your holy will as theirs. And what was seen as fearful now becomes a source of innocence and holiness.*
> *(ACIM; Workbook; Lesson #190)*

The resurrection is this very decision for Divine Joy. Amidst all of our struggles, we can always choose a higher thought or a higher feeling. Giving up grievances, self-judgments, and feelings of victimhood are the shifts in our mind that need to take place so we may "resurrect" our consciousness. The grandeur of the resurrection is seen in this very shift. We all have this level of awareness as our highest benchmark of evolution in life. The miracles given to us are designed to lift us out of limitations and place us in the vibration of Absolute Love. We can enjoy this journey of awakening. It is nothing short of awakening into our Christ Self we share, in which miracles become natural expressions of this Joy. Miracles are everyone's right. Miracles are everyone's inheritance. Miracles are everyone's means for stepping outside the problems we have made up. It is a complete transcendence above the thought forms that made the problems in the first place. It is the Mind of the Christ, our real Mind, our "highest Mind," that comes to our aid in this invocation for this decision. Our number one responsibility is to accept the Atonement for ourselves and claim this Christ consciousness—*this miracle consciousness.*

The grandeur of the resurrection is something we all must find. We are destined to find this highest joining no matter how long it takes. It is expressed so well in the words of the Christ in *A Course in Miracles:*

> *It is almost Easter, the time of resurrection. Let us give redemption to each other and share in it, that we may rise as one in resurrection, not separate in death. Behold the gift of freedom that I gave the Holy Spirit for you. And be you and your brother free together, as you offer to the Holy Spirit this same gift. And giving it, receive it of Him in return for what you gave. He leadeth you and me together, that we might meet here in this holy place, and make the same decision.—So will we prepare together the way unto the resurrection of God's Son, and let him rise again to glad remembrance of his Father, Who knows no sin, no death, but only life eternal. (ACIM; Text; Chapter 19; Section IV; ¶17)*

The grandeur of the resurrection is our own Easter time. We honor the birth of the Christ in ourselves, and this could be any day, any time, any year, and even any lifetime. We forgive all things, all people, and all aspects of ourselves that fell short of realizing our truth in the past. We claim our Self-Identity in this present moment because that is the only time there is.

I say, "Why wait to be who we truly already are?" True *resurrection* is in joining with our brothers and sisters as well, not merely in keeping resurrection for ourselves. We bring them along in this decision. We include all in this unification of our Higher Self to embrace the Christ in each person we meet—in every encounter of our day, and in every word of all our conversations. The grandeur of the resurrection is this absorption into our Creator as the Created, and loving our brother as ourselves. We are the "holy Son of God Himself." This transcends all lower orders of being which do not serve us anymore. Now we are the Christ. We are resurrected at this moment, and we have all the tools of forgiveness and the Atonement to maintain this Holy Awareness of our Divine Connection to our True Self.

25. Constant Happiness

Happiness is a feeling of well-being. Perfect Happiness is a deeper feeling of Peace and Joy. It is an elation of the Spirit that is not affected by the external and remains a constant state of being that is God's Will for us to have. If "God's Will for us is perfect happiness," and nothing else is God's Will for us, then it would follow that constant happiness is our only Divine Destiny to have. Whose happiness is constant? This vow to have *unconditional happiness* is mentioned in Michael Singer's book called *The Untethered Soul:*

> *Once you decide you want to be unconditionally happy, something inevitably will happen that challenges you. This test of your commitment is exactly what stimulates spiritual growth. In fact, it is the unconditional aspect of your commitment that makes this the highest path. It's so simple. You just have to decide whether or not you will break your vow. When everything is going well, it's easy to be happy. But the moment something difficult happens, it's not so easy. You tend to find yourself saying, "But I didn't know this was going to happen. I didn't think I'd miss my*

> *flight. I didn't think Sally would show up at the party wearing the same dress that I had on. I didn't think that somebody would dent my brand-new car one hour after I got it." Are you really willing to break your vow of happiness because these events took place?*
>
> *Singer, Michael A. The Untethered Soul: The Journey Beyond Yourself (pp. 142-143). New Harbinger Publications. Kindle Edition.*

Mr. Singer puts the challenge very well. Probably of our own accord, we would have trouble maintaining this vow. But who is making this vow? Our ego or the Christ Self in us? The ego has a long string of broken commitments that makes any vow feel impossible to keep. Are we using this "self" to make this vow? Christ has the certainty that "God's Peace and Joy are mine." This is the certainty we need, especially when we are making a vow for unconditional, or *constant happiness*. Are we using our Christ Self *in us* to make this vow of constant joy?

"Determination" is a factor in making any "decision." We need another energy to say "no" to a self-destructive habit. When we let go of the "payoff" or the "neurotic benefit" from keeping a destructive tendency, then we are well on the way to accepting this vow of "perfect happiness." A "payoff" would be something like this: I may "get sick" to receive more attention from family or my mate. I may "fail" because I am lazy and do not want an "added responsibility" that comes with success. These "payoffs" have to be let go of if we are to be in the vibration of *constant happiness*.

I am determined to see things differently.
(ACIM; Workbook; Lesson #21)

and,

Heaven is the decision I must make.
(ACIM; Workbook; Lesson #138)

The purpose of life is to be happy and have everything flowing in ease without effort. To shift our focus away from that which is not working for the betterment of our situation is to be "determined to see things differently." This kind of dominion over our mind is needed to maintain the vow of constant happiness. Rather than looking at the evidence of negative results and doing a post mortem, reaching for the antidote of positive thoughts and feelings is what the miraculous holds out for us. This is a practice required of us, as we have been trained to look at "what is" and pick apart all the things that have "gone off."

> *Creation knows no opposite. But here is opposition part of being "real." It is this strange perception of the truth that makes the choice of Heaven seem to be the same as the relinquishment of hell. (ACIM; Workbook; Lesson #138)*

We have to get this point. Heaven is the only decision to make. To "decide" for the things in our life that do not work out, correction is needed immediately. Shifting focus back upon the positive aspects of our life is essential. Dwelling on the things outside of Pure Joy will just give us more of those things. In the Mind of the Christ, the "hell" of our negative results does not even exist in the reality of possibilities.

But you might say, "I was just diagnosed with cancer. Are you trying to tell me that it does not exist?" OK. This is an extreme case of a call to "change your mind." The first step is forgiving yourself for all the negative "thought-forms" that contributed to the ailment. Some you know you have, and you have to let go of them. Many of these negative thoughts were lodged in the subconscious mind and you did not even know you had them. It is not even so important that you know what they are, but that you forgive yourself completely. And you forgive everyone else toward whom you may still hold grievances. The "treatment" then is thorough. It is corrective on the mind level.

In this way, the "personal hell" we made up is undone. It is a process of dissolving it with the power of forgiveness and in this case the most loving healing approach to any serious ailment. In conjunction with any medical treatment, we must cure the non-forgiveness in our mind as well. Cancer is a battle between the life force and the death urge—so anyone with cancer has to decide for life. Heaven is the decision we all must make, and also patience in undoing the mental mistakes we made in our manifestation of disease in the first place. Forgiveness is all-encompassing:

Forgiveness offers everything I want.
(ACIM; Workbook; Lesson #122)

Can we completely embrace the true meaning of forgiveness? The past is gone. The future is not yet. And the present, in which we all abide in this very instant, is clear and clean of all grievances. We are absolved of all errors, which means we absolve all others in our life from their errors. Our innocence shines in the originality of our Divine creation. We *decide* for Heaven and do not allow anything short of constant happiness to intrude upon our peace. If we have any "problems" in our life we trust that our commitment to a Divine resolution will gradually clear them up, even a stubborn disease, or a financial debt. We fully invite the Energy of God's Unconditional Love and care to take over our life. We are certain it will come to help. All the mistakes we made in the past are resolved. We take full responsibility for them, and we are also deserving of their correction. We are no longer a victim of any negative circumstances or situations beyond our control. The Divine in us is in control. We are gentle with ourselves and know the power of Love can overcome all the tinges of doubt or sadness that may remain in us. We are completely forgiven now, as everyone else in our hearts and minds are forgiven as well.

In this space of complete forgiveness, as mentioned in Chapter 9, we are given the *Gifts of God*. I will conclude this book by reminding ourselves of them again, as they are so important to infuse into our consciousness (and even memorize them so we can bring them to mind anytime):

"The Gifts Of God"

1) Peace
2) Happiness
3) A Quiet Mind
4) A Certainty of Purpose
5) A Sense of Worth and Beauty That Transcends the World
6) Care
7) Safety
8) The Warmth of Sure Protection Always
9) A Quietness that Cannot Be Disturbed
10) A Gentleness that Never Can Be Hurt
11) A Deep Abiding Comfort
12) A Rest So Perfect It can Never Be Upset

We may think these gifts are too ephemeral to have any meaning in our life. But Jesus assures us they are the real *Gifts of God* and the only ones that have real meaning because they are Absolute states of Being that align us with our Divine Destiny, our *real purpose for being here*.

Do we value them above all else is the question? When He says *Peace*, are we in that state? When He says *Certainty of Purpose*, are we aware that Joy is our main purpose in Life? When He says Happiness, do we have that unequivocally? To have a *Gentleness That Never Can Be Hurt* we would have to be kind and harmless ourselves. Are we harmless? Are we gentle? When it comes to *A Rest So Perfect It Can Never Be Upset*, are we there? Can we ever be upset? I think we can see we need a little work here. But all the Help is provided when we make these gifts our top priority to receive. We can always go for the Highest Thought, which is a Divine Thought that feels the best in our body and everyone around us agrees. The purpose of our life is to be supremely happy—and spread this Pure Joy to those around us in whatever form that brings us more Joy. We are an ever-flowing spring of Pure Joy then. We are "Drinking the Divine" and we know it. Our thirst is quenched, and our Pure Joy quenches the thirst of others. What could be better?

We have accepted these *Gifts of God*. They are in our bones. They are in our blood. They are in every Thought we think with our Divine Creator. We are in the flow of our own Creative Spirit and everything we do brings us higher into our real purpose for being here. We are not only aspiring to be in the values of the Christ, but we are also the Christ. I am the Christ. You, my reader, are the Christ. And we are extending this unconditional Love to the world we made up—to that world that needs our unconditional and complete forgiveness. All our "mistakes" have been corrected. We have accepted the Atonement for ourselves, and see that the mistakes were merely part of a dream of the "self we made up," which was not even the total picture of Who we are, in truth.

My eyes, my tongue, my hands, my feet today, have but one purpose—to be given Christ to use to bless the world with miracles.
(ACIM; Workbook; Lesson # 353)

Our life purpose is to BE THE CHRIST. I do not mean to imply "be a Christian and renounce any other religious background" within your past. The CHRIST, in this case, is not a "religion." You can keep all of that. If you are Muslim, you can "see the Christ" was very active in Muhammed. If you are Buddhist, "The Christ" flowed through Buddha's universal awareness that He taught and practiced. If you are from the ancient Indian religion of the Santana Dharma, you can recognize the clarity of the Absolute in the words and actions of Lord Krishna. Many enlightened beings have walked this planet in the Absolute state of Divine Love. None of them are diminished—rather, they are seen in the true light of Who they are. They are the Christ, and so are we in our acceptance of our true Self-Identity.

We stand together, Christ and I, in peace and certainty of purpose. In Him is His Creator, as He is in me.
(ACIM; Workbook; Lesson # 354)

Can we stand in the true Self-Identity of the Christ, together, you and I, and bring the much-needed shift in human consciousness more prevalently in our lives and the lives of those around us? This is our work to do. There are palpable rewards. We will receive the Gifts of God and make them our reality? Do we want Absolute *Peace*? Christ in us gives it. Do we want *A Rest So Perfect It Can Never Be Upset*? Christ has that too. Do we want a *A Sense of Worth and Beauty That Transcends the World*? Complete forgiveness offers this. If we stand with the Christ we must be as the Christ. This is a Law. This is a *Union of Absorption into My Creator as the Created*. (Odes to the Divine Mother, Ode # 301; bit.ly/DMOdes). We all came to end the separation we have felt over the eons between ourselves and God, between ourselves and the Christ, our real divine nature as a pure Human Being of God. And we can make this step Now.

What do we have to lose? We have everything to gain. No sacrifice is asked of us, but to give up our fear of doing so:

I gladly make the "sacrifice" of fear.
(ACIM; Workbook; Lesson #323)

To admit to ourselves that there just may be a higher state of being in which we are destined to live may be a great leap of faith, but it does not require we sacrifice anything of real value. Instead, it requires that we rise in fearlessness; that we ascend into a value of ourselves that is far greater than anything we have known before. We are lifted out of the doldrums of relative thought and life that has been ridden with pains and problems. We enter into the Absolute Life of our True Self that has totally transcended all problems and abides in a state of Constant Happiness. The only block we have is fear or the "belief" in our self-imposed limitations. Are we ready to make this leap of faith together? You, my readers, have come this far with me. Nearly 200 pages of discussing *The Second Coming* has led us all here. What are we going to do with this focus of our attention; our holy instant of release?

Certainly, the dragons of fear shall not get the better of us. They are mere movie projections on a screen of fantastic illusions. Doubt should be undone by now, given what has been shared so clearly up to this paragraph. Nothing has changed, and yet, everything has changed. Have we given "our eyes, our tongue, our hands and feet" to the Christ to "use to bless the world with miracles?" This is our responsibility through complete forgiveness to do so. He can help us make this step forward in our human evolution, but He cannot take this step for us. We must do that. We have to forgive ourselves and everybody, no matter what the past looked like; no matter what mistakes were made. We have free will to do that. And we also have free will to not do that—and keep recreating our various scenarios of unhappiness. A friend of mine once defined free will: "God gives us the free will to cause ourselves to suffer." That's pretty clear. One is never a victim again of anything after really hearing this truth.

This is a book about *The Second Coming*. This is a commentary on *A Course in Miracles* that brings this about. This is a book about us all rising up in our particular evolution as a soul to be as we are as God created us to be together—the

Christ. This is a book about giving up all lower orders of being that do not serve us anymore. We seek to know our wholeness now, in this One Life we share in total gratitude and delight for the perfect happiness that is God's will for us. We may still have healing to do, but we know we can do it in the innocence and peace that we are:

> ***Sickness is but another name for sin. Healing is but another name for God. The miracle is thus a call to Him.***
>
> *(ACIM; Workbook; Lesson # 356)*

Can we all make this "call to God" now? This is our birthright. This is our rightful inheritance to have total alignment with our Divine Creator, our Source of Life, with our Divine Father, Mother, Child as ONE—our Spirit, Mind, and Body as One Holy Entity as the Christ, which is Who we are.

We are well-grounded in the *Gifts of God*. We know what they are and we claim them through total forgiveness of the Atonement, the "correction of all of our past mistakes." There is no "retribution" required of us. There is no "debt to pay" that would "right the wrongs" we committed in the past—other than our total forgiveness of ourselves and all *others* together. There are no "others," as they are mere reflections of our own vibrational field. We clean up our act and leave others alone. We clean up our act and they will come into alignment with their True Self as God created them to be. All will be uplifted by our certainty of being. We do humanity a great service in our ascension.

The great sage, Henry David Thoreau, one of our spiritual "founding fathers" of the true American Spirit, said in so many words about serving humanity: "The greatest gift a man can give to his fellow-men is to rise to the height of his own being." Essentially he was saying, be the Christ in whatever form that takes for you. In his case, he had a profound love for Nature in which he could make contact with his transcendental Self. In the very order of the Universe that presented the Natural World around him, he found not only the Cosmic Divine but also his Divinity that was his expression of Heaven on Earth. We all must do this. We all must "rise to the height of our own being" within ourselves. What is this for us? It is our most pressing question in life to make good use of our time here in this physical dimension. We make our life meaningful and well applied in a state of constant happiness. And this has all-pervasive effects.

When I am very still and silent within, even the sounds and sights around me are woven into this tapestry of Divine Awareness. A car driving down the street is included in the silence. A bird that flies into the bush outside the window is part of the stillness. Stillness and Silence envelop all movement and sound into themselves. This is what I mean by "all-pervasive" effects. By the same token, when my mother passed away I was in the room with her. I had been holding her hand for about 6 hours straight. When she finally passed I was sad, of course. I felt my immediate grief—that was natural to feel—yet enveloping her and me was a deep sense of gratitude, and deep and lasting joy to be her son, and to embrace her in the Constant Happiness that was God Given in the moment. So you see, Constant Happiness is bigger than our setbacks, our sorrows, our "deaths in life," and our dynamic movements of the different periods and phases that make up the full unfolding of our lifetime here. Constant Happiness is as certain as the sun coming up in the morning; as the rain falling downward to cleanse the earth; as the fruit coming on the tree to sustain our life with Divine Providence.

If we are having a problem with a situation or an illness, we can call upon the immense Forces of the Divine to help us with it. And we assured we have the Help and the Answer when we are allowing it to come to our aid:

I need but call and You will answer me.
(ACIM; Workbook; Lesson #327)

My Father gives all power unto me.
(ACIM; Workbook; Lesson #320)

and,

No call to God can be unheard, or left unanswered. And of this I can be sure, His answer is the one I really want.
(ACIM; Workbook; Lesson #358)

What are we calling for? What is this "Power" God gives to us? What is the answer we really want? *The Second Coming* of *A Course in Miracles* is basically saying to all of us who touch it, read it, and apply its meaning in our life:

You are the Christ.

To the degree we do not accept this fact in the form of our Holy Self, we are denying our Self-Identity. We are still bound in the "prison cell" of the separated ego that we have made for ourselves. This ego maintains this gap between who we "think we are" and who we desire to be as God created us. Unfulfilled desires are not "hellish" and "painful" because they are desires, but because they are "unfulfilled." And they are not "unfulfilled" because they are wrong to have or because we do not "deserve" them, but because we are blocking them with our unwillingness to accept ourselves as the Christ, our fully aligned Self. This Self is already in us, already in the abundance of the Divine Flow. But we have to claim our Divine Self. When we start claiming the feelings of Constant Happiness that are the aspects of our true Self, then the desires that we have will start to be made manifest. And these ever-expansive attainments, fulfillments, add up to our Divine Destiny as the Christ. *The Second Coming* is then accomplished in us.

We have the Christ Self blazing its Holy Light of Truth and Beauty in every molecule of our Being, in every action of movement we take, in every gift of expression that pours forth from the breath of our Divine Being. We are Liberated and Free from the confines of any self-imposed unwillingness or artificial limitations of belief we have maintained in error before this moment of Total Awakening. We have God's Answer to our "problems" and it is the only one we want:

God's answer is some form of peace. All pain is healed; all misery replaced with joy. All prison doors are opened. And all sin is understood as merely a mistake.

(ACIM; Workbook; Lesson #359)

What could be clearer? It is like a crystal of ever shining rays of light into the reservoir of our accumulated holiness. It is what Esther Hicks calls our "escrow of vibrational reality." The Being of the Christ and all the miracles we will give through Him in us are already accumulated and lined up for manifestation in our world when we accept the Self God Created, not the limited one we made in an imagined "separation" from this Source of our Real Being—the one of Constant Happiness.

God does not want us to walk around in our life feeling limited and trapped in a body of pain and suffering—and eventually "dead." This is not God's will for us or our will for us. It is within our grasp in this lifetime to be totally liberated from these patterns of thought that keep us in the mediocrity of our "polite hells" that end in "death." There is no death. Only a passing from the physical to the non-physical dimensions of being. And even this transition is totally up to us in the time and space of this dimensional reality. We have "greater works to do," as Jesus told us we would have 2000 years ago. Are we ready to do them? Overcoming death itself is a pretty lofty purpose. Physical Immortality is possible. Do you want to fulfill this possibility in your life? You would need to "be the Christ" to do it. Are you ready? Are we ready to take up this banner of enlightenment together? We cannot do it alone, but we cannot be limited by the collective limitations and beliefs of lower orders of human concern. Above all else, do we really want to do this? "I want the peace of God," is Lesson #185. Do we? Do you? For with this Peace comes total liberation from death. Are we ready for this quantum shift in human awareness?

Peace and Joy engulf anyone who ponders the subject of being completely free—especially free of "death." We are "entitled to miracles." What would these look like to you? Let's state them here:

- I would like this to happen____________.
- I would like this to happen____________.
- I would like this to happen____________.
- I would like this to happen____________.
- I would like this to happen____________.

Imagine what it would be like to have these made manifest. These manifestations contribute to (but are not exclusive of) the Constant Happiness that engulfs your emotional life in an effulgent consumption of Peace and Joy. You deserve these things and they are here and now even though you may not see them. We rule our Minds, which are connected to the possibilities of infinite manifestation. In this field of the good, we are the Christ of our true Self, beyond any shadow of a doubt that we deserve to manifest our greatest potentials now.

There is no end to all the peace and joy, and all the miracles that I will give, when I accept God's Word. Why not today?
(ACIM; Workbook; Lesson #355

Let's release all unwillingness to accept God's Word. You are the Christ, joined with the Son of God Who was created at the foundations of Creation. You are the Light into which we all go eventually. Why not right now? Why wait? Do not delay. Do not waste time in dreams of sorrow or death—incarnate now into this Heaven on earth that is your place of true arrival. Accept the miracles coming to you. Accept the fact you are a Divine Child of God with all the power of God behind you.

We are all on a Divine Journey of awakening. This "place of our true arrival" is *here and now.* We all have our unique versions of Heaven on Earth, but for all of us there is but one all-pervasive quality of Constant Happiness that must accompany any version we envision. This must be for us and all those people around us. There "is no end to all the peace and joy," that we are entitled to receive when we are accepting of our true Self, the Christ. We share this Joy with everyone, even those enemies from whom we may feel separated. This is the Word of God made manifest in the flesh, in our flesh, right now. Can we accept it? Together we can. Together we can share in this Constant Happiness of Divine Self-Realization. And Christ leaves us all with a wonderful prayer for this moment, and for all moments henceforth:

> ***This holy instant would I give to You. Be You in charge. For I would follow You, certain Your direction gives me peace.***
> *(ACIM; Workbook; Lesson #360-365)*

In the realization of these directions is *The Second Coming* made manifest in us with a state of Constant Happiness.

Love,

Markus Ray

Epilogue

The power of decision is my own. This day I will accept myself as what my Father's Will created me to be.

Then will we wait in silence, giving up all self-deceptions, as we humbly ask our Self that He reveal Himself to us. And He Who never left will come again to our awareness, grateful to restore His home to God, as it was meant to be.

In patience wait for Him throughout the day, and hourly invite Him with the words with which the day began, concluding it with this same invitation to your Self. God's Voice will answer, for He speaks for you and for your Father. He will substitute the peace of God for all your frantic thoughts, the truth of God for self-deceptions, and God's Son for your illusions of yourself.

(ACIM; Workbook; Lesson #152)

Afterword

I hope this book you just read inspires you to continue to be a student of *A Course in Miracles*. I know that was Markus's intention. Every day I receive the blessing of being with a man (Markus) who lives *ACIM*. This makes such a difference in our marriage and in our lives in general. It is one thing to read it, it is another thing to live it. The challenge is in applying it. I know this book will help you with that. *ACIM* is all about how to be happy. It is all about how to be enlightened and have those two things go together—happiness and enlightenment.

For me, I was lucky enough to get the books around 1975 before they came out in three volumes to the general public. A friend sent me a Xerox copy of the first chapter of the Text in a big brown envelope and he wrote in red across the first page of the copy: "SONDRA, READ THIS IMMEDIATELY!" I am so grateful to that friend, as who knows how long it would have taken me to get the books if he had not done that.

I was raised in the Christian Church (Lutheran) and had to pass through the usual—baptism/ Sunday school/ confirmation school/ summer camps/ church college, etc. This was good and bad. The bad part was that a certain brainwashing occurred around the subject of sin and guilt, and heaven and hell. It was scary. It did not really teach me how to be happy. The worst part was that I was led to believe that if I questioned any of this, I would go to hell. You were supposed to swallow it all and accept it. One thing I could not tolerate was the fact that the church implied God was responsible for death. When I asked my Sunday School teacher why people in our little town had died, she said, "The Lord took them away." I was five. I protested and asked, "Are you trying to tell me God kills people?" She could not reply. Then when my father died (I was only 17) I found it intolerable to think God had killed my father. I was so upset that I ran away from the church college I was in at the time, moved to Florida to study nursing at the University of Florida in Gainesville, and married an atheist!

Since *ACIM* is a correction of religion, it was the only thing that could straighten me out and help me with overcoming this fear. For this I am supremely grateful. What if I had gone through my whole life stuck in the negative brainwashing of my church? I would never be where I am now. It takes time to unravel church dogma. *ACIM* is the most spiritual thing I can think of right now and you don't even need a church. I hope you accept this blessing for your own life. I hope your reading of *The Second Coming: You Are the Christ* by my husband Markus will take you to heights of your Being you have, until now, only imagined you could reach.

Love,

Sondra Ray

Benediction

Holiness is something we are immersed in whether we are aware of it or not aware of it. Why not be aware of it? It gives us endless joy. I am happy to have you in my life, my dear readers. You give me endless joy. We share in the holiness that we are. I am in the flow of the good tidings of *The Second Coming*. The only way to "fall out" of these good tidings, for any of us, is to not give our attention to them. Why would any of us want to do that? This is my first venture of writing a whole book on *A Course in Miracles*. It has been my wellspring of constant inspiration, and a cause for Constant Happiness. I have been a "student" of *ACIM* since 1985. I am "Drinking the Divine" of its wisdom every time I pick it up, and its holy water of Life never runs dry. It has been my great honor to write *The Second Coming: You Are the Christ*. I feel the hand of Tara Singh, my teacher of this great work, on my shoulder. I feel my own hand going out to rest upon your shoulders. May we rise together in this Holiness we share. May we be the Christ we are—together—that this world may be transformed. It is long awaited. Absolute Love is upon the planet, and may the worlds of our past no longer obscure it.
—Markus Ray—

About the Author

Markus Ray received his training in the arts, holding a Bachelor of Fine Arts degree in printmaking and drawing from the Cleveland Institute of Art, and a Master of Fine Arts degree in painting from the Tyler School of Art, Temple University in Philadelphia, PA, USA. Also a writer and a poet, he brings spirituality and sensuality together in these mediums of expression. He is the author of a major work, *Odes To The Divine Mother*, which contains 365 prose poems in praise of the Divine Feminine Energy. Along with the Odes are his paintings and images of the Divine Mother created around the world in his mission with Sondra Ray.

Markus is a presenter of the profound modern psychological /spiritual scripture, *A Course In Miracles.* He studied with his Master, Tara Singh, for 17 years, in order to experience its truth directly. His spiritual quest has taken him to India many times with Tara Singh and Sondra Ray, where Muniraj, Babaji's foremost disciple, gave him the name Man Mohan, "The Poet who steals the hearts of the people". In all of his paintings, writings and lectures, Markus creates a quiet atmosphere of peace and clarity that is an invitation to go deeper into the realms of inner stillness, silence and beauty. He teaches, writes and paints alongside of Sondra Ray, and many have been touched by their demonstration of a holy relationship in action. His iconic paintings of the Masters can be viewed on www.MarkusRay.com which he often creates while his twin flame, Sondra Ray, is lecturing in seminars.

Markus also gives commentaries and lectures on *A Course in Miracles* in live seminars with Sondra Ray and in his Miracles for You program—bit.ly/Miracles4You.

BABAJI, JESUS & THE DIVINE MOTHER

Sondra Ray & Markus Ray are brought together by the grace of their Master, Maha Avatar Herakhan Babaji. Babaji Himself said, "Markus is my Humbleness. Sondra is my Voice. Together they are my Love." As Ambassadors for Him, their mission is to bring His teaching of "*Truth, Simplicity, Love and Service to Mankind*" along with the presence of the Divine Mother to the world. They do so through seminars like the New LRT®, the healing practice of Liberation Breathing®, and the study of *A Course in Miracles*. They are unfolding the plan of Babaji, Jesus and the Divine Mother, Who provide a spiritual foundation for their worldwide mission of service. Their relationship is a shining example of what is possible through deep ease and no conflict. They can take you to a higher realms of being, where Spiritual Intimacy©, miracles, and holy relationships can become a big part of everyday life. Their major book on relationships they wrote together is *Spiritual Intimacy: What You Really Want With A Mate*. They offer private Liberation Breathing sessions over Skype, Zoom and in person, and various Seminars and Sacred Quests around the world. They work with Liberation Breathing® to help people free themselves from limiting beliefs and negative thoughts. They encourage people to discover more profound levels of *DIVINE PRESENCE* in their lives, and awaken more awareness of Immortal Love, Peace and Joy in their hearts.

Resources

The work of Markus Ray can be viewed on "Art Look—an art lover's companion." www.markusray.com You can also contact him there on that site, and sign up for his Art Look newsletter.

You can find Markus Ray's books on his Amazon Author's portal here: www.bit.ly/MarkusRay

Markus shares lectures, videos and commentary on *A Course in Miracles* with subscribers to "Miracles for You—1-Year Support Network" You can subscribe here:
www.bit.ly/Miracles4You

Markus has a Facebook page at:
www.facebook.com/markus.ray.169

You can reach Markus directly at:
markus@markusray.com

Twitter: www.twitter.com/markusray1008

Instagram: www.instagram.com/markusray1008

To Have a Liberation Breathing Session or consultation with Sondra Ray & Markus Ray, book one here:
www.bit.ly/LBSession

makusray.com/art-look

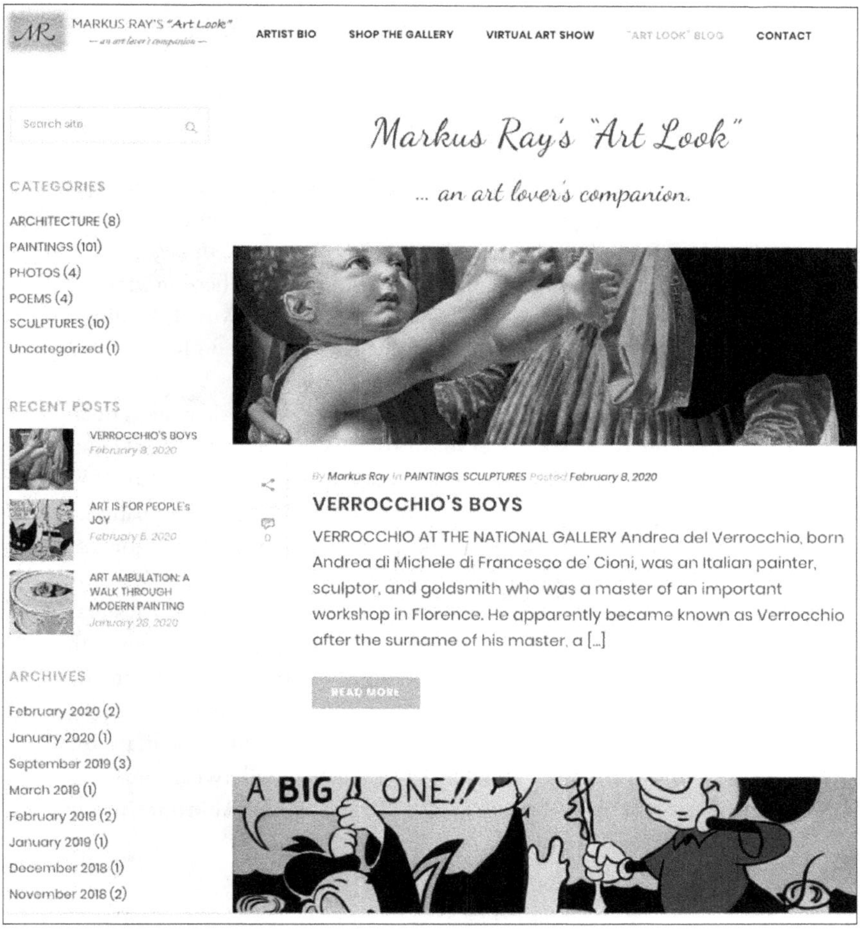
MARKUS RAY'S "Art Look"
— an art lover's companion —

ARTIST BIO | SHOP THE GALLERY | VIRTUAL ART SHOW | "ART LOOK" BLOG | CONTACT

Search site

Markus Ray's "Art Look"

... an art lover's companion.

CATEGORIES

ARCHITECTURE (8)
PAINTINGS (101)
PHOTOS (4)
POEMS (4)
SCULPTURES (10)
Uncategorized (1)

RECENT POSTS

VERROCCHIO'S BOYS
February 8, 2020

ART IS FOR PEOPLE's JOY
February 6, 2020

ART AMBULATION: A WALK THROUGH MODERN PAINTING
January 26, 2020

ARCHIVES

February 2020 (2)
January 2020 (1)
September 2019 (3)
March 2019 (1)
February 2019 (2)
January 2019 (1)
December 2018 (1)
November 2018 (2)

By Markus Ray In PAINTINGS, SCULPTURES Posted February 8, 2020

VERROCCHIO'S BOYS

VERROCCHIO AT THE NATIONAL GALLERY Andrea del Verrocchio, born Andrea di Michele di Francesco de' Cioni, was an Italian painter, sculptor, and goldsmith who was a master of an important workshop in Florence. He apparently became known as Verrocchio after the surname of his master, a [...]

READ MORE

A BIG ONE!!

Also See Markus Ray on Facebook
Facebook.com/MarkusRayArtLook

Other Books by Markus Ray

ALPHA OMEGA

The companion to SONDRA RAY's ***Lately I've Been Thinking***, Markus Ray compliments his wife's free flowing commentaries on Liberation Breathing / Breathwork, *A Course in Miracles*, Holy Relationships, and wisdom for day-to-day living. These guides for various Spiritual Quests to Sacred Sites around the world, continue their prolific output of written roadmaps to purposeful living.

Do you ever have a "dialogue" with yourself? Have you ever kept an ongoing journal of your everyday observations? Is your "start" and "finish" so intertwined they meld into just one thing of Pure Joy? ALPHA OMEGA is just that from MARKUS RAY— painter, author, and poet of "Odes to the Divine Mother." These journal entries from 2006 to 2009 form the basis of his commentaries on A Course in Miracles, his relationships with the Spiritual Masters, various life issues we all face, and his inner preparation to join with SONDRA RAY, his "twin flame," with whom together form the duo of a Holy Relationship. In this New Millennium made manifest, ALPHA OMEGA is a daily companion of freewheeling meditations, and a compendium of insightful tidbits that will tweak anyone's awareness of the First and the Last lesson of the Absolute in our everyday life.

AMAZON LINK: www.bit.ly/AORay

ALPHA
OMEGA
MARKUS
RAY
with Foreword by Sondra Ray

LIBERATION: FREEDOM FROM YOUR BIGGEST BLOCK TO PURE JOY

What is your biggest block to having Happiness all of the time? What's keeping you in a polite hell? Why has your life fallen short of Heaven on Earth? This book by Sondra Ray and Markus Ray will answer these questions for you, and provide the thread out of the labyrinth of your most negative thoughts in your subconscious that are sabotaging your life, or preventing you from going all the way to Pure Joy. Discover what they call a "Personal Lie," that is your most negative belief about yourself, hidden in the deep recesses of your psyche. Everyone has one to overcome. It is a main cause of all the things and events that went wrong in your life. Free yourself from it by reading this book, and practicing a few forgiveness processes.

AMAZON LINK: www.bit.ly/LibRay

LIBERATION
Freedom from Your Biggest
Block to Pure Joy
SONDRA RAY
&
MARKUS RAY

THE MASTER IS BEAUTIFUL

THIS IS A BOOK for you to have holy relationships directly with Spiritual Masters in your life. Do you want them? Markus Ray presents 9 parts in this book, each dedicated to a Spiritual Master who has greatly contributed to the eternal Wisdom of human spiritual evolution. He makes these Masters and their messages very accessible to the general public, in a way that can endear them to anyone interested in transforming themselves "upward" in their process of enlightenment.

Who would you invite to a holy banquet of the Wise? What would be your short list of dignified guests who had contributed the most to the enlightenment of your life? Author and artist Markus Ray puts together his exclusive “Master list” of those invited to his “last supper” of Spiritual Wisdom. You are invited too. Wouldn’t you like to participate in this celebration of the best and the brightest? Come along with Markus on this insightful journey to the feast of Absolute Love from these remarkable Beings.

AMAZON LINK: www.bit.ly/MasterRay

THE MASTER IS BEAUTIFUL
MARKUS RAY

PHYSICAL IMMORTALITY: HOW TO OVERCOME DEATH

This is a book that can permanently lift you out of despair, depression and hopelessness—a book that shows you how longevity is the linear result of quantum living.

Humans have something buried inside of them called an "unconscious death urge" which is our secret desire to destroy a body we feel trapped in. In this groundbreaking book, Sondra Ray teaches you how to dismantle the unconscious and hypnotic program (the unconscious death urge) which is literally killing you. The real tragedy of the unconscious death urge is not only that it causes us to die before our time, but that it generates resistance to a life of pure JOY. It makes life less attractive and therefore intensifies our desire to die and put an end to our misery. It's a vicious cycle.

This book is the solution that is 100% affirmative of life that offers a viable alternative.

AMAZON LINK: www.bit.ly/LiberationRay

PHYSICAL
IMMORTALITY
how to overcome death
SONDRA RAY
With
MARKUS RAY

BABAJI: MY MIRACULOUS MEETINGS WITH A MAHA AVATAR

This book may just blow you mind. The wild stories of a wild woman meeting her wild Guru in 1977, and all the stories of subsequent meetings afterwards. Unbelievable and true—off-the-charts encounters with Babaji, the Maha Avatar first mentioned in Yogananda's *Autobiography of a Yogi* in chapters 33 & 34—but in real life, in real time with Sondra Ray.

In her usual provocative style, Sondra asks her readers –

●What if you could know a Being who is not born of a woman and who could dematerialize and rematerialize his body? ● What if you could know a Being who is a major teacher of Jesus and who prepared him for his mission? ● What if you could know a Being who knows everything about your past, present and future? ● What if you could know a Being who can clear all of your karma? ● What if you could know a Being who is the sustainer of the universe, an ocean of knowledge? ● What if you could know a Being who is a never-failing spring of Bliss, the infinite essence of truth? ● What if you could know a Being who is the bestower of the highest Joy? ● What if you could know a Being who incarnated for the liberation of the world? ● What if you could know a Being who would fulfill all your desires?

You can know Him. This book is about Him. He says to you, "My Love is available. You can take it or not." Why not take it?

AMAZON LINK: www.bit.ly/BabajiRay

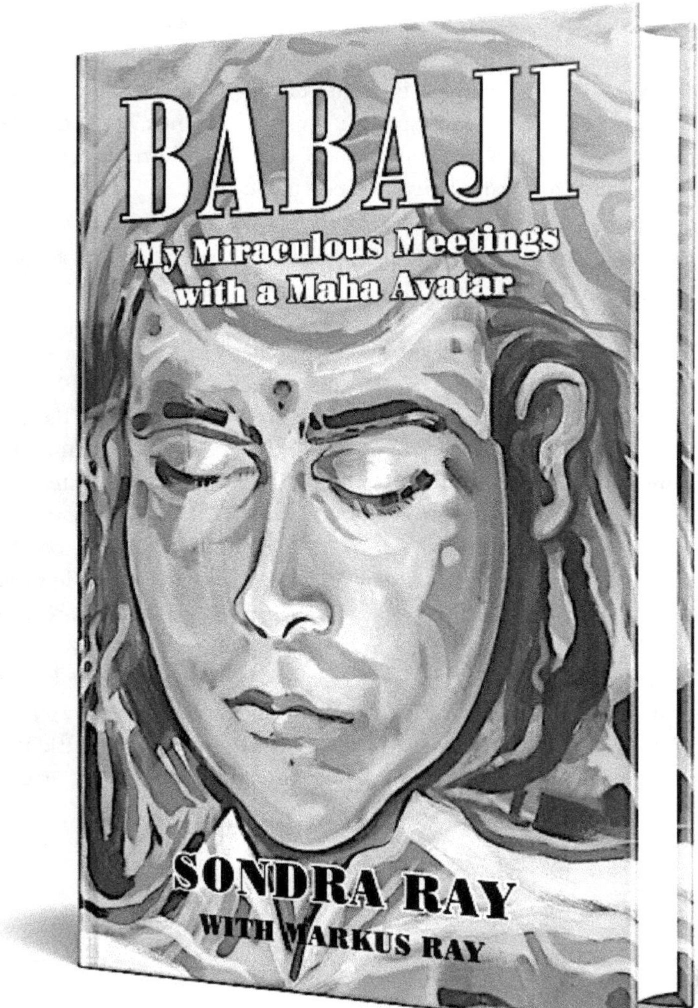
BABAJI
My Miraculous Meetings
with a Maha Avatar
SONDRA RAY
WITH MARKUS RAY

SPIRITUAL INTIMACY: WHAT YOU REALLY WANT WITH A MATE

What people really want in their relationships is deep connection, good communication, and spiritual intimacy. Sondra Ray and Markus Ray explore these common desires. They also give you 18 good ingredients that establish spiritual intimacy. And these ingredients permeate into all areas of your life, and transform them to embody truth, simplicity and love throughout.

Whether you are in a relationship or you are searching for that "right person," join Sondra and Markus to receive the benefits of living in the sacred zone of *Spiritual Intimacy: What You Really Want with a Mate.* Spiritual practices can get you in touch with your divine nature and help you stay clear of conflict and problems. Sondra and Markus give you simple approaches for integrating your spiritual life into your love life, leading to the possibility of Pure Joy! Examine the importance of Spiritual Intimacy in all aspects of your life- sex, money, parenting, career, and family life. Discover how true forgiveness, *A Course in Miracles*, and Liberation Breathing® combine to help you release the old paradigm that sabotaged your life in the past. Sondra Ray, the "Mother of Rebirthing", reveals how your birth trauma may be affecting your relationships, and what you need to do to clear it. Breathwork gives you breakthroughs. Enter the new frequency of Spiritual Intimacy for "something sacred" to enrich your life. More mainstream than tantra, more ecstatic than most spiritual practices, Liberation Breathing® is an experience every person or couple should try!

AMAZON LINK: www.bit.ly/IntimacyRay

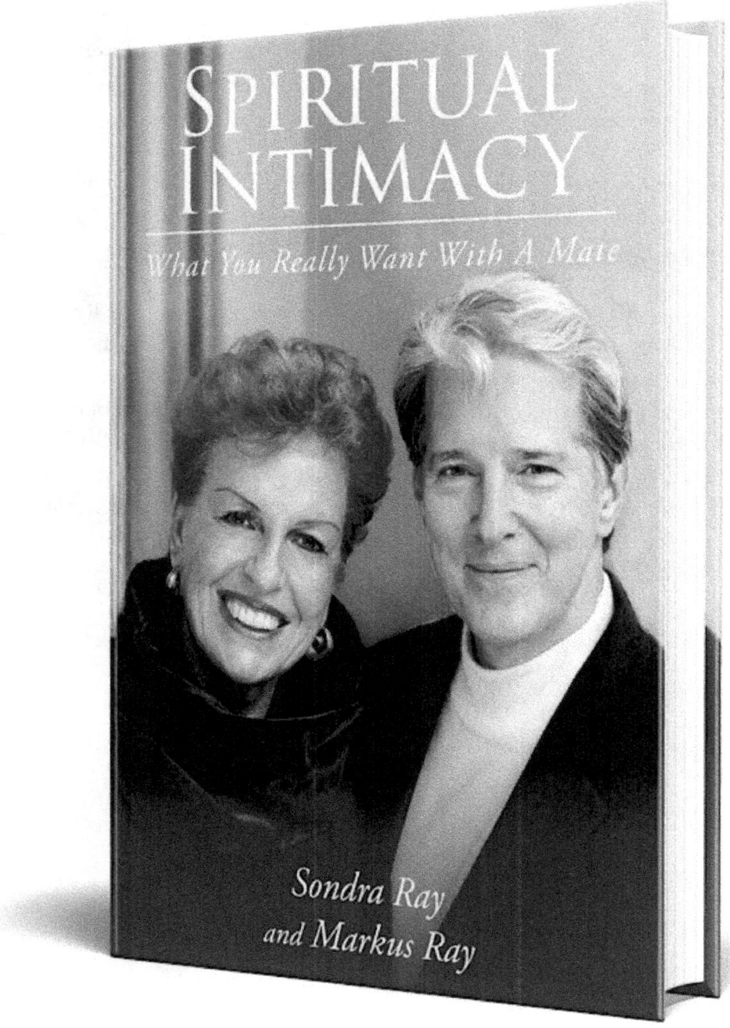
SPIRITUAL INTIMACY
What You Really Want With A Mate
Sondra Ray
and Markus Ray

ODES TO THE DIVINE MOTHER

Through intimate portraits and inspired meditations, Markus Ray cracks open the sacredness in coffee cups, mountaintops, airports, and vistas to reveal a Source that is divinely feminine. Infused with the essence of his lifelong study of *A Course in Miracles*, each page explores topics from ego and forgiveness to joy, Holy relationships, and Christ consciousness through daily dialogue with the Divine Mother. A sacred stillness emerges as one's consciousness opens— line by line to the purity, power, love, and perfection that is the Divine Feminine.

Markus Ray is a visionary painter, poet and teacher. He lives in Washington, DC, with his wife, author Sondra Ray. Together they offer seminars, virtual programs and Quests to sacred locations around the world, introducing thousands each year to Liberation Breathing®, The Loving Relationships Training®, and *A Course in Miracles*. Markus is the coauthor of *Liberation Breathing: The Divine Mother's Gift*. His paintings are featured at www.MarkusRay.com. Also see Markus Ray on Art Look —an art lover's companion— at www.bit.ly/ArtLook

AMAZON LINK: www.bit.ly/OdesRay

ODES to the DIVINE
MOTHER
MARKUS RAY

LITTLE GANESH BOOK

Solve all you problems with this book! In this collection of short aphorisms and meditations, Markus Ray pays homage to Ganesh—the Elephant God in Eastern mythology Who is the remover of obstacles. You can use them to inspire your day, and to remove the difficult hurdles in your own life.

A friend gave Markus a tiny Ganesh and he immediately loved it as it is pocket size. Therefore Markus always carries it with him. Knowing that Ganesh is the one who removes obstacles, I have seen Markus take it out of his pocket and set it on the counter, especially at airports. This was funny because I usually had my suitcases overweight so Markus was asking Ganesh to "handle that." I must say it very often worked! Ganesh is the Lord of success and destroyer of obstacles. This is the most popular deity in India. His large belly is an essential attribute. It is said to contain within all the universes, past, present and future. There are many legends as to why Ganesh has an elephant head. One explained that Ganesh was created by Shiva's laughter. —Sondra Ray—

AMAZON LINK: www.bit.ly/GaneshRay

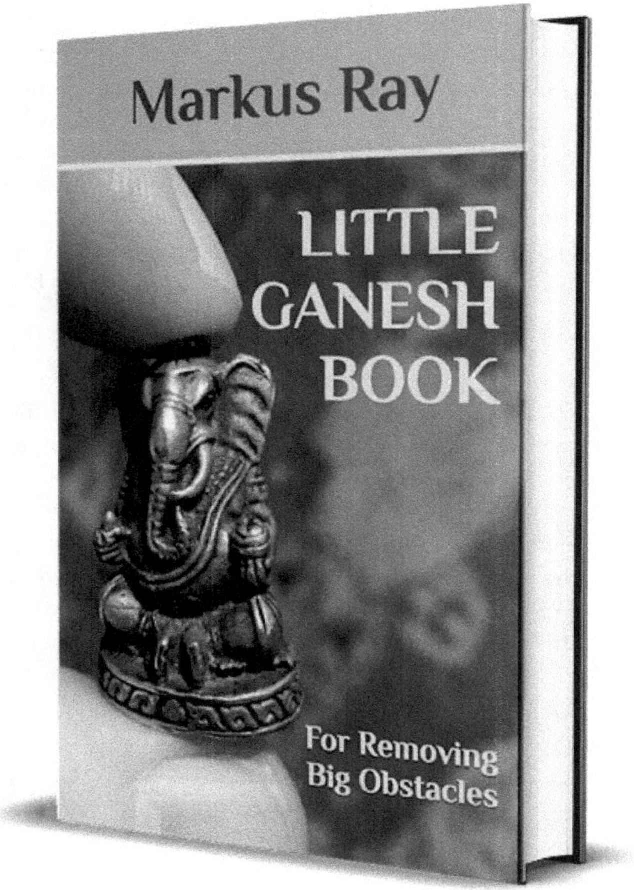
Markus Ray
LITTLE
GANESH
BOOK
For Removing
Big Obstacles

MIRACLES WITH MY MASTER, TARA SINGH

In this book, author MARKUS RAY comes forward to transmit to you the many blessings he received from his teacher of *A Course in Miracles*, TARA SINGH. This touching story of miracles, raising the dead, meeting the saints of India is compellingly and openly told within. MARKUS spent seventeen years studying with TARA SINGH from Easter of 1989 to March of 2006, and describes him as, "my life teacher, my spiritual guide, my Master, and my friend." TARA SINGH was guided directly and ordained by the scribe of *A Course in Miracles*, Dr. Helen Schucman, to give workshops and instruct serious students of this sacred, self-awakening course for enlightenment. His insights into the application of *ACIM*'s principles stand unrivaled, as written in *A Gift For All Mankind*, one of his major classics.

MARKUS says, "I wrote this account of those years I spent with TARA SINGH—our encounters, his teachings in my life, our travels and experiences together at home and abroad, and my own melding with the Presence of this great man—so other students of *ACIM* may receive the intensity of actual miracles in their study of this modern day scripture. Also, I desired to write an accurate complement to TARA SINGH's mission with *ACIM*, seen through the eyes of one of his students. These memoirs are a testimony of my gratitude for the miracles I witnessed in his Presence, as the main guiding light in my life."

AMAZON LINK: www.bit.ly/TSRay

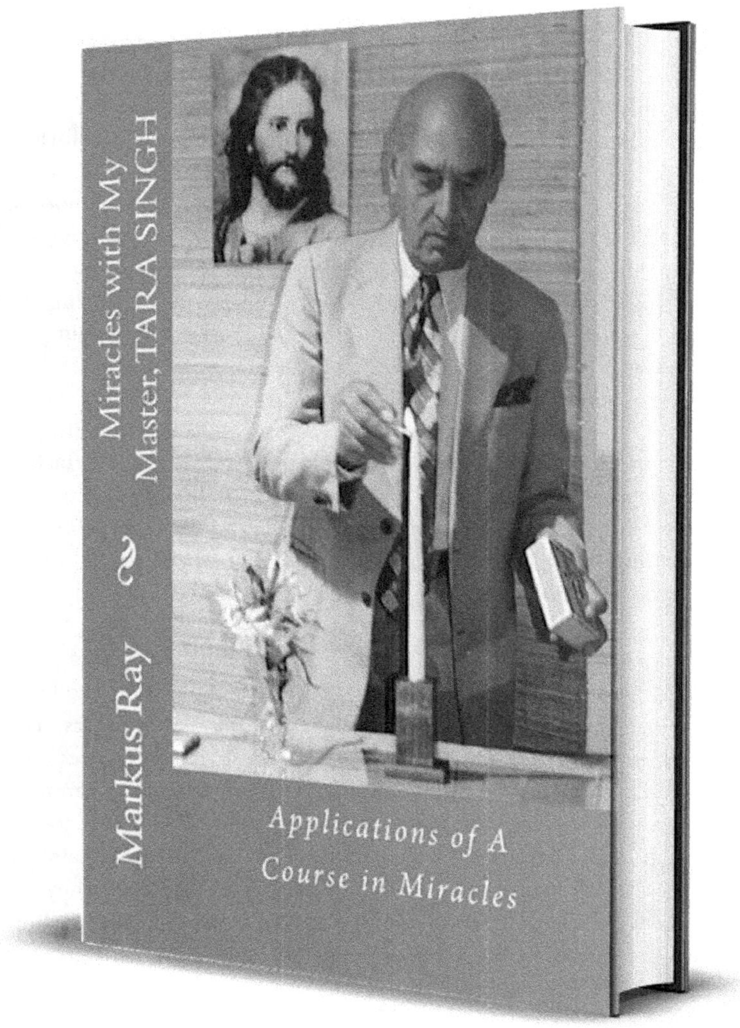
Miracles with My Master, TARA SINGH
Markus Ray
Applications of A Course in Miracles

LIBERATION BREATHING: THE DIVINE MOTHER'S GIFT

This is Sondra Ray's "Bible on Breathwork," a guidebook for expanding into life, spirit, and happiness through the power of your own breath. Discover how Liberation Breathing®—a form of breathwork practiced worldwide—transforms on the mental, physical, and spiritual dimensions. Sondra Ray's newest book on Breathwork elevates the soul while releasing readers from negative thoughts, traumas, and relationship patterns. Ray unites the power of breath with her extraordinary commitment to healing and miracles as she details the evolution of Liberation Breathing. She reveals how the breath cycle transforms the mind, body, and soul when coupled with self-inquiry, prayer, and affirmations. Through essays and case studies, she details the spiritual and historical influences of the modality while honoring its roots in the Rebirthing Movement. An instructor manual for breathwork practitioners, a guide for birth workers, and a rich source of information for those seeking personal transformation, this book is for anyone intrigued by the benefits of conscious, connected breathing.

Sondra Ray and Markus Ray merge their collective knowledge of breathwork with their passion for *A Course in Miracles* and the Divine to bring you the most salient teachings of the past 40 years. Their vast grasp of spirituality, prenatal psychology, the subconscious mind, health, ascension, aging, and the teachings of immortal masters result in elegant tools for releasing birth trauma, relationship patterns, grief, addiction, anger, physical pain, and disease, while increasing life urge and joy. Together, they take readers on an exploration of life, spirit, and bliss through the simple act of breathing.

AMAZON LINK: www.bit.ly/LiberationRay

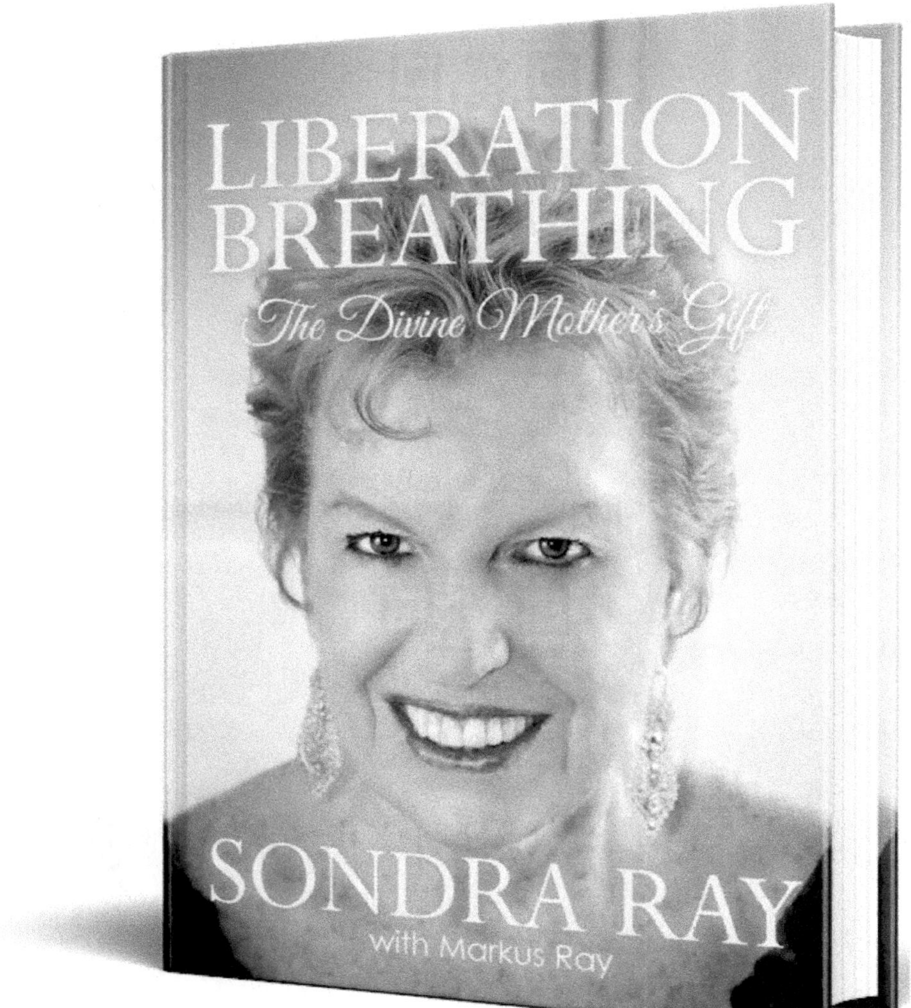
LIBERATION
BREATHING
The Divine Mother's Gift
SONDRA RAY
with Markus Ray

MARKUS RAY'S Author's Portal :

Bit.ly/MarkusRay

SONDRA RAY'S Author's Portal :

Bit.ly/SondraRay

Notes

Notes

www.ingramcontent.com/pod-product-compliance
Lightning Source LLC
Chambersburg PA
CBHW060255100426
42742CB00011B/1763